Fundraising Innovators

Leaders in Social Enterprise Share

New Approaches to Raising Money

By

Amy S. Quinn

www.FundraisingInnovators.com

Fundraising Innovators: Leaders in Social Enterprise Share New Approaches to Raising Money

ISBN: 978-1-935689-59-1

Published by Wise Media Group, LLC

Original 50 Interviews concept by Brian Schwartz

Cover Design by Patryk Sobczak

Interior layout by ePubTemplates.com

TABLE OF CONTENTS

Preface

Why Fundraising Matters

Operating any organization from a deficit is untenable. Yet nonprofits frequently face difficult budget choices, such as postponing necessary technology upgrades in favor of sustaining current programming. With today's continued economic uncertainty, nonprofits can no longer afford the luxury of operating from an ordinary paradigm. Many suffer chronic financial instability, which can undermine their mission and long term-viability. Indeed, fundraising matters, perhaps now more than ever.

Many well-known best practices in fundraising already address sustainability[1]. Today's leaders have access to many proven resources, such as those made available by the Association of Fundraising Professionals or *Chronicles of Philanthropy*. Yet the ideas in this book offer alternative approaches to amplify the proven fundamentals. *Fundraising Innovators* will introduce a host of modern approaches to fundraising in pursuit of sustainability.

At some point in our lives everyone learns to ask for money. Many volunteers struggle with this task in support of a given mission, such as supporting a school fundraiser. This book, however, is for professionals, particularly individuals in the following roles: Executive Directors[2], Gifts Officers[3], Corporate and or Gift Planning managers, Nonprofit Board Members, Foundation Leaders, and Brand Marketers. If you serve in the philanthropic space, these pages will introduce you to innovators and a growing network of Social Entrepreneurs that are shaping the future of modern fundraising. Come read what they have to offer!

My Journey to Writing this Book

After many years of involvement with a family nonprofit, I've acquired an appreciation for the dedication and values of fundraising professionals. My family was thrust into fundraising for spinal cord paralysis research when my brother was paralyzed in 1982. Although still motivated by our passion for a cure, we have grown

1

familiar with the relentless challenges of funding this ambition. So too, fundraising professionals work with extraordinary challenges that are acknowledged and addressed in this book. Their success impacts individual lives and our communities.

Nonprofits may struggle with significant headwinds, but visionary leadership and technological innovation are driving change in the fundraising field. Teaming with the publisher, *50 Interviews*, my goal is to introduce you to these leaders and the power of their ideas.

To garner multiple data-points, I identified membership and research-driven organizations such as Network for Good and the Nonprofit Technology Network (NTEN). I also searched for social entrepreneurs and corporate leaders serving our communities, such as CiviCore, Corporate Responsibility Magazine, Convio, Causecast, Giveo and Crowdrise. These pages include interviews with large nonprofits in health services, medical research, education, and social services (Teach For America, University of Denver, the Robin Hood Foundation and the Christopher and Dana Reeve Foundation); savvy consultants such as We First, Arquero Consulting and M+R Strategic Services also contribute.

The expert interviews provide the research foundation for *Fundraising Innovators*. For the most part, all interviewees were asked and responded to the same questions, allowing me to uncover common themes on the following topics: Technology, including Social Media[4], Integrated Marketing[5], Corporate Philanthropy, and Sustainable Best Practices. Subcategories include Donor Loyalty, Gratitude, Collaboration, Metrics[6], and Tried and True Business Principles.

Many interviewees spoke repeatedly about technology. In my experience, their passion is only equaled by the thrust most nonprofits have for the benefits of technology. My experience with technology includes leading a local "Tech4Good" chapter on behalf of NTEN and TechSoup. In the past year I have also participated in a ten-week online Tech Academy as well as a six-week webinar series, "Creating a Social Media Toolkit." In addition to my interviews, I have reviewed current literature on relevant nonprofit topics. Much of what is written can be correlated to current literature.

Savvy fundraising is needed for nonprofits to become self-reliant. Successful development work is often defined as closing transactions. Conventional wisdom assumes that once a donation is in hand, a goal has been met. Yet, as we'll learn from the interviews in this book fundraising today encompasses so much more.

Fundraising Innovators provides specific know-how to update foundational practices with innovative approaches. In the following interviews, you will find contemporary solutions to today's challenging environment. In this way, your organization will not only reach it's financial goals, but also become "modernized" in the process. Modern nonprofits are defined by sustainability, a prerequisite to achieving your mission.

4

Introduction – What's New in Today's Fundraising Environment

In concert with the opinion of most fundraising professionals, the innovators in this book echo a commonly understood challenge: "nonprofit organizations (NPO's) are undercapitalized, operating with one hand tied behind their back." Such pressures have only increased since the financial crisis of 2008. Donations during 2008 and 2009 decreased 13%. Although 2010 charitable gifts increased 2%, equaling $290.89 billion, they remain lower than 2007 levels.[7]

Financial struggles are not new. Nor are other traditional challenges within the nonprofit sector including; employee burnout[8], infrastructure gaps, regulatory scrutiny, redundant missions, and too few Major Donors[9]. Sometimes frustrations arise from founders who can get in their own way instead of forming partnerships. Too often nonprofits focus solely on procuring the corporate check versus focusing on the long-term relationship. With over 1.6 million[10] nonprofits in the United States, it is safe to assume that too many organizations provide the same service and chase after competing supporters.

TECHNOLOGY – TRAP OR TOOL?

Added together, these challenges are compounded by the rapidly evolving capabilities of technology. Technology, including social media, has fully arrived on the scene in 2012[11], affecting and deconstructing every aspect of an organization, including its fundraising. Although not a technology manual, this book and the leaders profiled in it, will address a full range of tech topics including software for managing constituents, website tools, e-mail, data capture, measurement capabilities, online marketing platforms[12], and social media.

When applying IT, many nonprofits remain in a "chaotic" and "reactive" state; no plan, in constant fire-fighting mode, and scant funding for immediate technological needs[13]. Technology has also drastically changed current marketing practices since now a consistent message must be delivered across a myriad of channels. In addition, younger generations and or the majority of individual donors expect online communication while older generations interact more with offline efforts, a new dichotomy in donor engagement.

DONOR DEMOGRAPHIC DICHOTOMY

Major Donors are aging. The average age of a million dollar donor is 76 years old. They will be followed by Baby Boomers[14] turning 65 or older (a demographic expected to grow by 35% in the next ten years). The wealth transfer to these Boomers will begin with individuals between the ages of 75 and 90 years old.[15] But waiting for the much anticipated wealth transfer is not a strategy, nor does it address the N-Geners (American under forty) and their philanthropic potential. Reaching this emerging group of young donors while concurrently nurturing relationships with Major Donors is a challenge addressed by those interviewed in this book.

MODERN SOLUTIONS

The innovators profiled in this book describe current and repeat challenges in terms of potential solutions, not problems. With their extensive leadership and entrepreneurial experience, they provide insights and practical strategies. As a group, they reinvent fundamentals and utilize current resources to solve problems. Taken together, these contemporary leaders use a modern approach to fundraising.

Modern denotes "current", "what's new" and or innovative. In addition, modern infers reinvented, examining what has worked in the past and distinguishing the best fundraising principle for today. How will applying modern principles, those which combine new with reinvented practices, impact your work as a fundraiser?

In *Fundraising Innovators* the interviewees reveal the following "How To's" to benefit your work.

6

How to:

- Leverage technology to enable mission
- Integrate marketing to engage the smaller donor while concurrently cultivating the Major Donor
- Champion corporate philanthropy and foster collaboration

The interviewees also offer strong revisions on familiar topics such as:

- Donor loyalty
- Board and employee management
- Strategic planning
- Marketing

MODERN EQUALS SUSTAINABILITY

The interviews in *Fundraising Innovators* reflect how fundraising today requires a contemporary approach, integrating innovation with reinvented fundamentals. By applying these new and updated practices, a nonprofit can raise more money and drive towards self-reliance. A modern approach translates to a strengthened nonprofit, one financially sound, meeting programmatic goals and effectively maximizing its resources, perhaps even through the formation of new partnerships with other nonprofits, corporations, foundations or government agencies.

Sustainable fundraising also means that the donor's motivations are matched to funding priorities while current technology enhances relationships, outreach and community. Internal departments propagate a consistent message with a willingness to examine the organization's strengths and weakness. Current leaders constantly work with their Strategic Plan within a progressive environment.

While The Great Recession[16] has forced many Americans to "soul search" and financially scale back, nonprofits too, should reflect on how to better sustain their organizations. Current economic uncertainty, fractured demographics, and new technology create the demand for an evaluation. In *Fundraising Innovators* the interviewees provide innovative and fresh answers for reaching fundraising goals. Consistently meeting financial benchmarks within a strategic plan creates independence. Becoming modern, therefore, enables sustainability and the consequential ability to fund programs and priorities. Sustainability is the goal. With it, nonprofits can focus on achieving mission, no longer distracted by inordinate burdens. Why else do nonprofits exist other than to solve the problems in our world? Following the contemporary recommendations in this book will benefit both the fundraiser and the nonprofit.

Getting the Most from this Book

This book is organized into five key pillars of modern fundraising:

1. **Leverage Technology**
2. **Integrate Marketing**
3. **Champion Corporate Philanthropy and Collaboration**
4. **Reinvent Fundamentals**
5. **Build Sustainable Practices**

In each chapter, you'll find interviews with those who share insights germane to each concept.

At the end of each interview, you will find *Discoveries* that came as a result of each interview. I suspect you'll have some of your own discoveries, and I encourage you to share them with your colleagues and other readers at:

www.FundraisingInnovators.com

Utilizing the *Key Take Aways* at the end of each interview will help you apply the concepts described to your own organization, now! I encourage you to put them on your calendar, share them with your team, and assign the necessary resources to implement them. Add them to your annual plan, bring them to your board, follow through to completion, and measure your results.

Shaded topics represent bonus material. These sections offer additional research or elaboration on topics discussed during various interviews.

Further elaboration on terms noted with an endnote throughout this book can be found in the Endnotes section.

As an added resource, in *Chapter Six – A Fundraising Innovators Action Plan*, I've created an action plan and resource list, a starting point for applying the concepts from this book, to your own organization.

Additional items of interest can be found in the Appendix, including *18 Leadership Principles of Fundraising Innovators*, A case study of *Zappos*, and an index of nonprofits mentioned in this book.

Quick reference to topics discussed in each interview:

	Katya Andresen (p. 55)	Vinay Bhagat (p. 17)	Richard Crespin (p. 86)	Steve Daigneault (p. 76)	Francisco Gonima (p. 111)	Peter Kiernan (p. 140)	Scott Lumpkin (p. 150)	Simon Mainwaring (p. 94)
Advocacy				X				
Behavior Economics (including Self-Interest)	X					X	X	X
Cause Marketing	X		X					X
Collaboration and or Shared Values	X		X	X	X	X		X
Corporate Giving and or Capacity Building			X		X			X
CRM Platforms and other technology platforms		X						
Donor Relationships, Prospects and Growth	X					X	X	
Gratitude	X							X
Integrated Marketing	X	X		X		X		X
Major Donors		X				X	X	
Metrics		X			X	X	X	
Peer-to-Peer and or Crowd Sourcing	X	X		X		X		
Revenue Sustainability	X	X			X	X		
Segmentation	X	X				X	X	X
Social Media	X		X	X				X
Strategic Planning and Leadership		X	X	X	X	X	X	
Technology	X	X	X	X				X
Transitions						X		
Transparency				X		X	X	X

	Ed Messman (p. 36)	Rich Rainaldi (p. 66)	Holly Ross (p. 28)	Ryan Scott (p. 103)	Eric Scroggins (p. 131)	John Shaw (p. 187)	Hank Stifel (p. 159)	Peter Wilderotter (p. 120)	Robert Wolfe (p. 45)
Advocacy									
Behavior Economics (including Self-Interest)		X		X	X	X	X	X	X
Cause Marketing	X			X					
Collaboration and or Shared Values			X	X	X			X	
Corporate Giving and or Capacity Building				X		X	X		
CRM Platforms and other technology platforms	X	X	X	X					X
Donor Relationships, Prospects and Growth	X	X	X		X	X	X	X	
Gratitude	X	X	X				X		
Integrated Marketing	X		X						X
Major Donors					X		X	X	
Metrics	X		X	X	X		X		
Peer-to-Peer and or Crowd Sourcing				X				X	X
Revenue Sustainability	X			X	X			X	
Segmentation	X		X						
Social Media	X		X	X					X
Strategic Planning and Leadership		X			X	X	X	X	
Technology	X	X	X	X	X				X
Transitions								X	
Transparency	X			X	X		X	X	

11

Chapter One – Leverage Technology

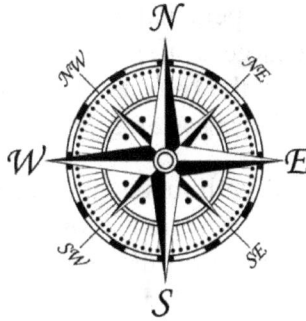

Admit it! For many of us over forty, technology represents an enigma to unravel. It's broad-reaching and, at times, can be confusing. In addition, we feel pressure to participate in social media as represented by occasional or even frequent use of Facebook, LinkedIn, Twitter and YouTube. Sheepishly, this was my view until asking my interviewees: *"How has Technology and social media changed fundraising and how might organizations maximize opportunities associated with these technologies?"* Their answers reiterated not only the importance and potential of embracing technology in the nonprofit sector but in my own career as well!

First, we must define technology being used by the nonprofit sector. In this chapter, Vinay Bhagat, Founder of Convio, describes technology in four primary categories including (1) constituent tracking and analytics, (2) website delivery, (3) transaction capabilities and (4) e-mail functionality. The interviews in this chapter also discuss the use of technology tools for fundraising and engagement campaigns[17], crowd sourcing[18], social media, and market segmentation.

While social media is only one component of technology, it has, tremendous potential to elevate a nonprofit's level of engagement. Interviewee, Simon Mainwaring, founder of We First consulting, feels that technology, and specifically social media, has brought humans together again:

"Technology is teaching the world to be human again. Like donors, consumers want a better world and will utilize social media to support or rally against a brand."

Katya Andresen of Network for Good further explains: "(social media) is a platform for personal expression…as marketers and fundraisers are not in charge of the message anymore. To me, the promise of social media is the peer networks and the idea of friends fundraising and sharing their passion for a cause."

Are there rules associated with this engagement? Can we truly have transformative conversations and community online? Those interviewed in this chapter uniformly say "yes," that the Internet and technology have provided a democratization of communication. The opportunity to build community using technology across the globe does exist! Further, utilizing technology is also about improving operating efficiencies and program delivery. If technology is maximized, it can differentiate an organization and it's mission.

In this chapter, Vinay Bhagat, Holly Ross, Ed Messman and Robert Wolfe will examine how nonprofits leverage technology, in alignment with their strategic goals, to engage donors, define programmatic benchmarks and enable fundraising success.

Leveraging technology means climbing the pyramid

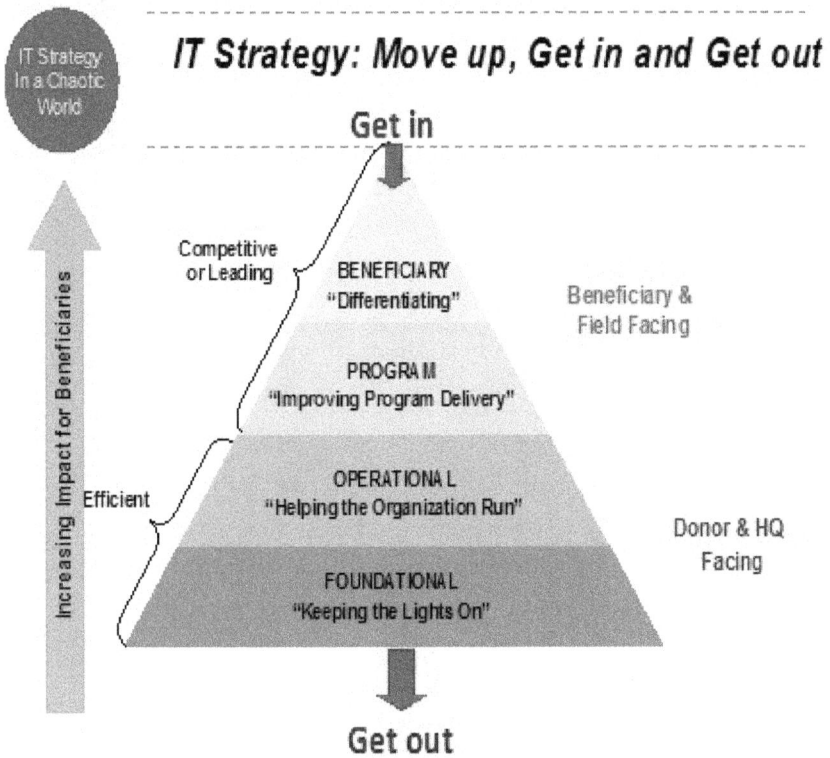

Pyramid Graphic from Edward G. Happ, Global CIO and Head of ISD, International Federation of Red Cross and Red Crescent. http://eghapp.blogspot.com/ (reprinted with permission) [19]

Vinay Bhagat: Embracing Technology and Its Tools

"If well designed, technology should empower and build capacity.[20] It should not be overly complex, nor difficult to use. When properly implemented, technology is pervasive enough for everybody to access, creating an amplifying effect in terms of organizational efficiency."

-**Vinay Bhagat**, Founder and Chief Strategy Officer, Convio, Inc.

Themes
Technology, Constituent Management Platforms, Strategic Planning, Integrated Marketing, Metrics

Profile
Established: 1999
Listed: NASDAQ Global Market under symbol CNVO
Location: Headquarters in Austin, TX
Number of Employees: 440
Revenue (2010): $69.5 million
Money Raised Online (2010): across all clients: $1.3 billion
Clients: More than 1,500 nonprofit organizations globally

Description of Business
Software As a Service[21] Provider of Constituent Engagement Solutions for nonprofit organizations. Convio has two primary

17

offerings. The first, *Common Ground*, offers an all-in-one, easy-to-use donor engagement system for small and medium-sized nonprofits.

The second offering, *Luminate*, is for larger nonprofits and is comprised of Convio's i "enterprise-class" CRM[22] with highly scalable multi-channel analytics and campaign planning solution.

Mission: To connect people with causes to achieve extraordinary results

Background

Vinay Bhagat's favorite quote is from Mahatma Ghandhi, "Be the change you wish to see in the world." Since founding Convio in 1999, Bhagat and his team have steadily built Convio into a healthy, global company, greatly changing and scaling technology in the nonprofit sector. In 2008, Convio entered the donor management/CRM category through a partnership with Salesforce.com. At that time, Salesforce.com, the leading Software as a Service commercial CRM software company had made their platform available to nonprofits free for less than ten users and heavily discounted for more than ten users. Instead of reinventing the wheel, Convio decided to build upon the Salesforce.com CRM platform and extend it into a fully-fledged fundraising solution for the nonprofit sector. This strategy has allowed Convio to quickly deliver robust offerings to the nonprofit sector. It also has meant that the ecosystem of application and service providers surrounding Salesforce.com have become available options to many nonprofits.

Vinay has many well-deserved accolades: in 2006 he was named Fundraising Professional of the Year (on the agency side) by *Fundraising Success Magazine;* in 2004 he received honorable mention as one of the top 25 people worldwide changing the world of the Internet and Politics. He frequently speaks at industry conferences, and is a widely published author. As with others interviewed for this book, one of his favorite business books is: *Good to Great* by Jim Collins.

Vinay feels that technology should align effectively with process and goals. All too often a nonprofit might believe that hiring a Major

Gift Officer is the best way to expand fundraising capacity. If aligned strategically, Vinay asserts, technology can better build capacity and efficiently take a mission to scale up[23], more than any individual hire.

In his interview, Vinay also provides advice on marketing, believing nonprofits can differentiate themselves through effective integrated marketing – leveraging and coordinating different channels and programs to lift performance for the organization as a whole – building stronger relationships and optimizing marketing spend.

Interview

From a technology perspective, what are the absolute basics that must be in place before any nonprofit can successfully fundraise for a cause?

Technology needs to facilitate and enable good business processes. While "basics" vary depending upon an organization's scale and sophistication, there are some common denominators. First, every organization needs tracking capability for constituent interactions, whether they're donors, volunteers, clients, advocates, etc. Ideally the Customer Relationship Management system should not just be a depository of information but rather helps orchestrate a constituent development plan.

In this day and age, a strong website is an imperative. Donors, including Major Donors, frequently visit websites before making a contribution to a new organization and first impressions count. A website must effectively convey a nonprofit's value proposition, how it differentiates itself, demonstrate clarity around how funds are used, and have the capacity to accept online donations (both one-time and recurring). Ideally online donation forms should support honorary and memorial giving, and since Major Donors do occasionally give large gifts online, forms should be able to accept large transactions without limits. Increasingly organizations are offering options to donors to direct funds, and if possible, those capabilities should be manifested as online donation options. Returning donors should be recognized and their contact and billing information pre-filled. In some cases, organizations may elect to also pre-select "ask strings" presented based upon a returning donors last or highest contribution.

All nonprofits need the ability to communicate via email and increasingly social media channels. Ideally those email capabilities should support personalized messages to constituents, recognizing them not only by name but also presenting content of most relevance/interest to them. Email technology should also support the ability to provide a responsive experience for supporters in scenarios like an automated receipt or reminder the day before an event.

Increasingly, nonprofits should also consider some kind of peer-to-peer fundraising capability to harness the reach and willingness of supporters to fundraise from friends and family. Our *Next Generation of American Giving* research indicated that peer to peer solicitation is the most acceptable form of solicitation across ages, but particularly so with younger donors.[24]

Aligning Technology with Business Strategy –

The Miracle Foundation

Vinay and his wife are supporters of an Austin-based organization called The Miracle Foundation, which funds orphanages in India. Initially, the Executive Director focused on Major Gifts, which required a basic database management system. As the organization expanded, adding smaller donors, volunteers, running fundraising events etc..., it created the need for a more robust CRM system. As they added a monthly sponsorship program, it necessitated technology for increased website credit card payment capabilities. As the organization harnessed existing supporters reaching out to others, it added a social or peer-to-peer fundraising capability. Vinay has been using the peer-to-peer fundraising system to raise money from family and friends, in honor of his late grandfather. As a small organization, all of these technologies need to be easy to use, well integrated and economic. Technology has enabled The Miracle Foundation to scale, diversify beyond Major Donors, drive stronger donor loyalty and build a broader support base.

How do you recommend nonprofits prioritize their technology?

It all starts with strategy! Often nonprofits make technology decisions when they haven't determined a strategy that defines exactly what they are trying to accomplish, what the key priorities are, what marketing/fundraising strategies they should pursue, and hence what system and human resources are required to accomplish their goals. Moreover, in larger organizations, technology is sometimes bought without a full comprehension of the work required to drive system adoption and business process change.

How do you feel technology has changed fundraising?

The Internet and technology has dramatically changed fundraising over the last ten years. Ten years ago, less than $250 million was raised online. Last year, Convio alone handled $1.3 billion in donations. Moreover, email communications, the Web and now social and mobile have dramatically changed how donors are recruited. Sophisticated integrated marketing groups are raising more than 25% of mass marketing funds online, and event based organizations sometimes more than 75%. Organizations adopting and effectively implementing CRM technology have found efficiency gains in how Major Gift Officers work, in managing programs, and in providing donor service. The advent of software delivered via the Internet i.e. software as a service, has also made capabilities more accessible and affordable.

However, just like every sector, there are "early adopters" and "laggards" (terminology from Geoffrey Moore's *Crossing the Chasm*[25]). Many "laggards" are stuck in the "I have a donor database and a website" era i.e.: using a database only for simple contact management, versus strategic fundraising capability, and not harnessing the potential of the Web. Unfortunately, legacy technology present in some organizations inhibits adoption because of its complexity.

Many believe the way to scale fundraising operations is to add a human being: "If I have X amount of spare dollars, I will spend it on a Major Gift Officer…I wouldn't buy technology." Technology, however, should be able to help you scale beyond what a human can do, like maximizing your in-house staff and leveraging volunteers.

Peer-to-peer fundraising is a good example of how technology has changed fundraising. Over the last two years there has been a shift in how constituents react to marketing messages. They are less susceptible to direct marketing messages and, instead, more receptive to hearing from family, friends and co-workers. Peer-to-peer fundraising enables volunteers to tell a nonprofit's story or perhaps their personal connection to the cause.[26]

How might nonprofits better maximize their technology versus feeling overwhelmed by it?

If well designed, technology should empower and be viewed as a capacity enabler. It should not be overly complex, nor difficult to use. When properly implemented, technology is pervasive enough for everybody to access, creating an amplifying effect in terms of organizational efficiency.

For organizations that are intimidated by technology, add a board member and staff who are comfortable and fluent with it. But, be wary of building in-house technology versus buying what's already readily available, off the shelf.[27] Focus on your core competency instead. There are long term costs associated with maintenance and reliance on an individual or firm.

From a marketing perspective, when you look at the nonprofit community, which organizations are doing the best job differentiating themselves and why?

Organizations must be willing to take risks in their marketing campaigns to differentiate themselves from the noise we receive as consumers. Here are just a few examples of larger organizations that differentiate themselves:

Charity Water has built a tremendous brand by clearly embracing technology from the start, understanding the power of social media and a simple consistent message.

Since rebranding itself a couple of years back, Feeding America has kept marketing messages on target, utilized strong images and made appeals very tangible for donors to understand their potential impact.

PETA (People for the Ethical Treatment of Animals) has effectively segmented their marketing strategies for different audiences from Generation Y to Boomers. They have also been "Early Adopters" in the social media and mobile marketing space.

On a smaller scale, Austin based Mobile Loaves and Fishes (MLF), a social outreach ministry for the homeless, has demonstrated some bold marketing tactics. Recently, the founder, Alan Graham, conducted a multi-channel campaign. During one facet of the campaign, they put a homeless person called Danny on a billboard with a sign behind him reading: "Text Danny to 20222 and he'll be $10 closer to getting off the streets" or visit the campaign's website.

What are your recommendations for creating an integrated marketing program?
To most, integrated marketing means integrating across channels. For some, it also means integrating across programs (convert donors to activists and activists to donors, for example). At a macro-level, integrated marketing requires a leadership commitment to setting internal goals that create collaboration while allowing a donor to choose their preferred giving and engagement channels. Internally, functions should not be penalized if a supporter switches channels. Furthermore, organizations should align organizational structure to support integration, e.g. integrating online and offline marketing teams under one leader, for example.

Instead of examining metrics and response behavior in only one channel, success metrics should encompass all channels and assess long term donor value, aka, "lifetime value." This means shifting from the single analysis of an individual campaign, like response to a direct mail solicitation, to analyzing the long-term impact on lifetime value (frequency of giving, retention rate etc.) for a particular "treatment" strategy, or series of communications/engagements across channels.

In addition to examining monetary value, it's possible to create an engagement score that factors advocacy participation or the opening and forwarding of an e-mail, or posting on a social network, for example. While charities focus on whether someone has made a donation, the future lies in measuring quantitative engagement that looks beyond fundraising and helps predict the propensity to give.

(*Author's Note: According to a 2007 research paper presented by Convio and an analytics firm, StrategicOne, a multi-channel marketing approach improves donor lifetime value, regardless of whether a donor makes a contribution online or not. Supporters who donate online in addition to responding to a direct mail solicitation have even higher lifetime values. Therefore, it makes sense that an analysis needs to assess the whole effect of multi-channel communication over the lifetime giving cycle of a donor.)

Integrated Marketing Metrics

According to a recent white paper conducted by Convio and Edge Research and authored by Vinay Bhagat, (Integrated Multi-Channel Marketing: Where Nonprofit Organizations Are Today & Key Success Factors Moving Forward, 2011), many organizations are tracking integrated marketing metrics that "measure key phases of the donor lifecycle across channels." These metrics include: New Donor Acquisition, Donor Value By Channel, Donor Channel Migration, Cross-Channel Contact Information and Donor Retention.

What do you believe is the key to loyal donor relationships?
Donor loyalty is dependent upon being constituent–centered: delving into what's important and interesting to a supporter, determining how best to correspond, and what the preferred channels of communication are. It means recognizing that individuals are motivated by different things. For example, in our Wired Wealthy research[28] a couple of years back, we learned that some very generous donors are quite business like in terms of how they want to be communicated to (financial reports, donation receipts etc), versus others who want a much more emotional dialogue. Even smaller organizations with a mass communication model need to still understand their audiences.

How might nonprofits become more self-sustaining?
Nonprofits might attempt to promulgate two types of funding. First is the opportunity to increase the use of a monthly sustainer program. Second, contingent on the type of nonprofit, examine alternative revenue generation models and create an earned income stream. A little "out-of-the-box" thinking might yield earned revenue sources.

Third, harness the power of volunteers. Technology can help. Many volunteers have the human capacity to actually deliver on the mission. Mobile Loaves and Fishes, a social ministry that serves the homeless, for example, has over 10,000 volunteers that drive trucks, distribute food etc... and help spread the word. If charities harness an individual's natural passion for a cause, volunteers can also help fundraise. In our case, my wife and I recently made a significant gift to the Miracle Foundation, in honor of my grandfather. I am now reaching out to my family and friends, to encourage them to contribute too.

Charities need to see themselves as a vehicle for the donor as opposed to seeing only a checkbook. As Alan Graham, the founder of Mobile Loaves has said: "Yes, we feed the homeless, but we are not a homeless charity. We are a vehicle for people to exercise their faith to contribute."

What do you know now as a leader that you wish you had known sooner?
The success of an organization is determined by what occurs at the grassroots level. Front line workers need to feel passionate, empowered and knowledgeable and aligned in terms of standards of operation and a company's goals. As the organization grows, certain standards around ethos and philosophy will scale as well. Good management isn't enough: there needs to be emphasis on a consistent culture in the organization. When pervasive, the culture becomes self-reinforcing allowing the organization to be healthy and successful on all fronts.

It's also important to have an open and candid culture that encourages people to think for themselves and speak up when something is broken. Instead of a top-down oriented culture, it should be a blend between leaders setting strategic direction and front-line employees feeling motivated to make it all happen.

How do you define innovation in the nonprofit sector?
Innovation comes in different forms, in operations, funding, marketing, and program models. Kiva[29] and DonorsChoose[30] have radically re-thought the philanthropy model by connecting the donor online to the recipient or project. Other organizations, like Live Strong, Charity Water or the Michael J. Fox Foundation for

Parkinson's Research have been online-centered from the start, and, therefore, less reliant on traditional fundraising channels like the mail.

Convio measures innovation in terms of the effective use of the web and technology in driving mission and fundraising success. We focus on the marketing aspect of innovation versus program-delivery. Each year, we select 10 clients as stand-out examples of innovation in different categories, and recognize them through Innovator Awards.

Discoveries

- When designed correctly, technology should empower and be pervasive; accessible to all employees in the organization. It should be viewed as a capacity enabler and, if prioritized correctly, should enable an organization to scale beyond what one person can accomplish.
- Nonprofits who have successfully differentiated themselves in marketing understand the power of social media and a consistent and simple message. They know how to segment their strategies for different audiences.
- "Integrative" marketing means integrating across channels. It means a leadership commitment to internal collaboration while externally providing donors with the ability to choose their giving channel.
- Metrics enabled by technology should assess lifetime donor value across all channels and include quantitative measurements of engagement.
- Charities need to see themselves as a vehicle for the donor to give back, not just a service provider who will cash their check.

Key Take Aways

- Examine your strategy to determine how technology will be prioritized in the organization. For organizations intimidated by technology, add staff and or board members that are comfortable and versed in it.
- A strong website conveys a value proposition to the donor and clarifies how money is spent. Online transaction

capabilities should work for multiple types of gifts and might also include the ability to direct funds as well as embed "ask strings" based on a donor's giving history.

- Regardless of an organization's size, craft appropriate e-mail messages for audience segments.
- Consider a "Monthly Sustainer" program or alternative revenue-generating source for creating a recurring sustainable financial model.
- Peer-to-Peer fundraising is a good example of how technology has changed fundraising and provides current opportunity to the nonprofit. Many constituents, including volunteers, react more positively to their peers talking about a cause than traditional direct marketing messages. Does your organization use Peer-to-Peer fundraising?

Holly Ross: Integrating Technology with Marketing

" Organizations stand out when they have a very clear sense of "who they are" and evenly reflect their image across all the different communication channels."

-Holly Ross, Executive Director, Nonprofit Technology Network

Themes
New Digital Technologies, Online Marketing, Transparency, Metrics, Donor Recognition.

Profile
Type: Nonprofit
Location: Portland, Oregon
Members: Large and small nonprofits, technology consultants and vendors providing technology tools

Description of Services: "NTEN facilitates the exchange of knowledge and information within our community. We connect our members to each other, provide professional development opportunities, educate our constituency on issues of technology use in nonprofits, and spearhead groundbreaking research, advocacy, and education on technology issues affecting our entire community."

Mission: "Where the Nonprofit Technology Community Meets! NTEN aspires to a world where all nonprofit organizations use technology skillfully and confidently to meet community needs and fulfill their missions."

Background

In 1999, Holly Ross started working for Tech Rocks, an organization focused on technology in advocacy[31] work. Holly says that her prowess in Excel made her work noteworthy because, at the time, most professionals still used paper forms while she pushed the more logical approach of spreadsheets and e-mail. With e-commerce just beginning, people noted Holly's savvy.

When Holly joined NTEN in 2003, she directed its first showcase event, a conference that focused on the use of technology in the "doing good," nonprofit arena. Today, NTEN continues to bring people and resources together. During her interview, Holly provides a fresh outlook and offers a high technology edge to her answers. Her commitment to maximizing the best use of technology by nonprofits is striking.

Interview

What community does NTEN serve and how do you serve them?
While our primary focus is purely on the Information Technology (IT) side of an organization, over the last two years, we've expanded to include marketing and communication programs, specifically supporting Executive Directors and fundraisers. Our membership is a mix composed of three groups: nonprofits, technology consultants that serve the charitable industry and vendors that provide the tools. Across the nonprofit spectrum, we have very small members with budgets under $500,000 to mega-sized establishments, like the American Red Cross. Technology needs vary within this space.

When you look at just the nonprofits, which organizations do the best job differentiating themselves in terms of their marketing and why?
Organizations stand out when they have a very clear sense of "who they are" and evenly reflect their image across all the different communication channels. With so many communication avenues, it's challenging to achieve consistency. Campaigns can be excessive, encompassing direct mail, website, email, Facebook, banner ads, TV ads and more! Successful nonprofits integrate their online and offline strategies with inordinate clarity.

Have you seen any successful collaboration between nonprofits sharing a similar mission?

Over the last five years, the weak economy has indirectly mandated the need for more collaboration between nonprofits. "Collaboration" has been an important word in our sector. We've seen an increase from funding organizations (i.e., foundations) requesting joint funding of a program to the benefit of more than one organization.

How does NTEN foster collaboration?

Most common is our collaboration through the co-hosting of webinars or research studies with partner organizations, like M+R Strategic Services, a consulting firm specializing in advocacy, government affairs and grass roots campaigns. We've also had joint opportunities through some of our internal programming. Last year we shared our retreat theme and location with a bigger organization, The Georgia Center for Nonprofits (GCN). While GCN created the programming for the leadership track, we programmed the IT Staff, Communications, Fundraising and Programs tracks. Both sets of members benefitted from attending either type of session. Also, we have a few board members serving both our organization and other like groups, such as TechSoup.

What do you feel are the absolute basics that need to be in place before an organization can really successfully fundraise for a cause?

The first basic is to make sure you have the right person in place for the fundraising job. In the IT world, there is a tendency to hire someone with enthusiasm and strong personal qualities but not perhaps the skill set for the technology job. I suspect this occurs in fundraising, too. If unsure, consult with fundraising experts and or board members on how to evaluate the necessary skills and conduct a thorough hiring process. Don't let your own ignorance result in a bad hire.

In online fundraising, measurements must be established before launching a campaign and, then, thoroughly measure effectiveness and success through its completion.

What's been the most successful online campaign you have seen for raising money and what was unique about it?

After the Haiti earthquake, the American Red Cross (ARC) clearly demonstrated success with its digital technology. Through its text messaging campaign, ARC raised over 30 million dollars, five and ten dollars at a time, representing a 14% response rate.[32]

ARC's well-known brand and huge scale partly explains their success. We might assume that with a 14% response rate, similar to direct mail results, a texting campaign is much more efficient and easy.

After the Japanese Tsunami we witnessed another innovation; the use of ATM machines as an easy way to donate. In this case, there was not a direct ask. Rather, donating to the American Red Cross became part of a client's daily integration with technology. The simple process of giving was combined effectively with the current emotional impact people felt at the time.

Our current thinking around core fundraising practices has changed. In the future, giving will occur at a point of integration with our daily life, a way that is convenient. Instead of pushing a broad marketing message the organization will tether an emotional response with a digital channel tied to our everyday life, like our ubiquitous cell phone.

Does an 80-20 rule apply to digital fundraising? In other words, do 80% of the gifts come from 20% of the donors?

Although we do not have enough consistent data, Target Analytics Group[33], a software and data consulting company, conducted a study of online fundraising results from twenty-eight large organizations. First-time donors trended toward higher donations than those acquired from other channels but response rates overall were lower. Online donors also did not repeat their gifts year over year at the same rate as a donor acquired from another channel. This lack of loyalty shows itself in other online giving venues as well, such as Facebook's Birthday Wish, a giving opportunity about the birthday gift and not necessarily the cause.

On the other hand, Epic Change, an advocacy nonprofit, has had fundraising success by maximizing its relationship with a smaller online group. It embraces a rule in social media called "1-99:" 90% of followers will be mainly inactive, 9% somewhat active, and 1%

extremely active. Epic Change commits to the 1% in online engagement, seeking to interact and build an extremely strong community with this core group. The donor experiences a much more targeted and impactful interaction than with the customary large outreach.

What do you think is the key to loyal donor relationships and how can you develop these relationships online?
NTEN's work understands the importance in appreciating donors and making them feel part of something big. In fundraising it's crucial to communicate clear specifics about what funds support. For example, Epic Change not only tells the donor exactly how the money will be spent, especially when a campaign begins, but continuously engages donors along the way. They report on the thermometer movement, reflecting back to the donor, "Look what you helped us achieve." Epic Change directly asks for input and philosophies around associated issues, elevating engagement to an even higher level.

We know that scale affects the results of online fundraising, that 1% of a "gagillion" followers will translate into a beneficial dollar amount. With Epic Change, we've learned that it's possible to work with a smaller segment online and be just as effective in raising funds. This means that large organizations can narrow their marketing and online programs, and instead of reach, re-focus on the donors that show loyalty. In a couple years potentially the technology will allow us to more closely examine our most loyal donors.

Are you saying that technology allows you to segment your donor base?
Yes, organizations, like the Humane Society, already segment their online constituents. When someone requests information about cats, the contact information is tagged for felines and not dogs! Consequently, this client will receive future marketing e-mails about cats. Interacting at the right interest level will build the relationship with the donor.

How has social media and technology changed fundraising?
One of the most fundamental changes as relates to technology is transparency. With current technology, consumers expect

32

information on demand, requiring nonprofits to act transparently in all behavior. In addition, consumers have the ability to communicate negatively when expectations are not met in a timely manner. Responsiveness becomes extremely important, especially with the use of Twitter. The bar for presenting an organization's analytics will also be raised as more and more organizations operate openly.

What are the basics for effectively using technology?
Start with your website, the epicenter for online fundraising. In an extremely clear, well-organized manner, a website should present a strong impression of management, provide an easy way to make a donation, include financial performance and an explanation of funded programs. A sharp website presentation facilitates a donor's decision to give, or not.

Also, consider the back-office experience, after a donor makes an online donation. Who internally receives the information and how will it be analyzed? How quickly is a thank you sent?

How do you feel corporations should support philanthropy?
We're seeing a shift in public perception of who does "good" in society, whether it's a social entrepreneur, a nonprofit or a corporation. Corporations are also opening more to the idea that the bottom line is not the only indicator of success. Rather, there are societal obligations too, like environmental or philanthropic impact. Although I recently read an article that espoused a 1% donation of earnings to corporate charities, I feel that we should encourage multiple models; any way that brings the corporations into the charitable space, like Wells Fargo's willingness to create ATM donations. All types of partnerships are possible and it's important not to define corporate participation by dollars alone.

How might charities become more self-resilient?
According to *Forces for Good: The Six Practices of High-Impact Nonprofits* by Leslie R. Crutchfield and Heather McLeod Grant, high performing nonprofits operate concurrently at many levels, working in "grassroots" below and advocacy above, solving the problem while shaping the sector. It's important that nonprofits understand their impact as an individual piece, in addition to their affect on the whole puzzle. Let's look at a food pantry established to solve hunger. The problem is not only about distributing food.

To solve hunger, the food pantry should be aware of what's happening at the job training center or the homeless shelter. Collaboration, in the sense of sharing data with one another, will lead to a better understanding of the issues surrounding hunger, thereby utilizing resources more effectively and indirectly fostering self-resilience.

Are there some business disciplines that should be incorporated into fundraising? Why or why not?
As I mentioned earlier, measuring results as a basic practice is key. In addition, nonprofits should analyze their business processes and or how they complete their work. In online fundraising some nonprofits have invested in a new tool, hired staff and then, ultimately, found out that the strategy did not work. Since they didn't invest enough time nor evaluate the process in advance, their investment was wasted.

What do you know now, as a leader, that you wish you had known sooner?
Not coming from a fundraising background, I initially became distracted by overanalyzing the right process to solicit. Although good planning is essential, at the end of the day, you have to ask people to donate.

Do you have a mantra at NTEN?
"Listen" is central to how we operate here. In order to meet our members' needs, we must hear what they say.

Discoveries

- There's been a shift in the definition of who does "good" in society, whether it's a social entrepreneur, a nonprofit or a corporation.
- Giving will occur at a point of integration with our daily life, a way that is convenient and tethers an emotional response with a digital channel (e.g. text messaging).
- With inordinate clarity, a nonprofit's image must be communicated consistently across online and offline marketing channels.
- Although scale affects online fundraising, reach does not always translate to effectiveness.

34

- Too often, nonprofits focus solely on their one issue and do not examine the big picture.

Key Take Aways

- When seeking grants, consider a joint effort with synergistic nonprofits.
- Share data, retreat themes, webinars and research studies with complementary-focused nonprofits to better maximize resources.
- Follow the 1-99 Rule of social media; Commit to the 1% in online engagement, focusing on those donors that show loyalty.
- Don't define a corporate partnership by dollars alone. How might you expand your corporate relationship?
- Establish clear metrics for fundraising campaigns and always analyze the results.
- Explore giving opportunities at a point of convenience, within a donor's daily life.

Ed Messman: Online Campaigns

"Why would you message somebody who is twenty-five, no kids and unmarried the same way you might market to an individual who is married, has children in college and is fifty years old? The same offer doesn't make sense!"

-Ed Messman, Founder & CEO, Giveo

Themes
Technology, Metrics, Donor Segmentation, Online and Offline Marketing, Transparency, Breaking the 80/20 Rule[34]

Profile
Type: Social Entrepreneurship
Location: Boulder, CO

Clients: Pennzoil, AEG, Denver Museum of Nature and Science, Denver Post, Davis Phinney Foundation, Denver Botanic Gardens, F3 Foundation, 9 News, Haiti Partners, Flobots, Brooklyn Community Foundation

Description of Business: Giveo is the only hosted data marketing platform that combines continual consumer data enrichment with innovative applications to run higher performing campaigns across web, social, email, and mobile media. Combined with the right support from our marketing services team, Giveo helps marketers deliver on the brand, cause, and direct marketing objectives set by their organization.

Mission: "Our ambition is to advance public/private partnerships that deliver big social impact."

Background

In late 2007, Ed Messman worked for HiveLive who offered "white label"[35], social software platforms to businesses. At the time, there was a proliferation in the use of social media. Users were becoming more comfortable with consuming, buying and communicating online with friends. JP Lind, Co-founder of Giveo, had launched the nonprofit group at Epsilon Marketing and helped the country's top nonprofits with their direct marketing initiatives. Messman and Lind felt that, in the near future, consumers, especially the younger demographic, would utilize social media to engage with charities. Messman and Lind created a company to take advantage of this opportunity.

Strong analytics are at the core of any campaign's success. During his interview, Ed Messman shares his prolific knowledge for creating digital marketing campaigns, those built on reliable metrics. For Messman there's no waffling: it's mandatory that nonprofits embrace the revenue balancing and resource optimization that comes with strategic digital marketing.

Interview

Who are your clients at Giveo?
Giveo serves the greater "cause community" which includes nonprofits, corporate and community foundations, and for-profit brands. Our marketing focuses on the unique attributes of the marketer within nonprofits, foundations and corporate brands.

What services do you provide?
We provide a subscription to our platform of "white label" applications. The platform is highly configurable, deployable and offers a creative design to leverage and extend an existing brand's

assets. Brand extension is actually a big differentiator and creates deeper customer loyalty.

Throughout our multiple offerings, we identify the objectives for engaging and or finding new constituents. We also establish measurement frameworks in how to use marketing dollars and or assess fundraising efforts. Strategic goals might include:

- Identifying existing audience and discovering more insights on who they are and how to best target them along with the current competitive landscape;
- Defining opportunities for bringing an attractive campaign to market;
- Developing creative design and the configuration of digital marketing solutions;
- Launching a campaign and measuring its outcome.
- Campaigns are highly targeted to reach constituents that not only "raise their hands" but also have a specific demographic and transactional profile.

How does Giveo define Cause Marketing[36]?
Cause marketing starts with the nonprofit and its cause, not the other way around. If you start with the brand, efforts will bleed into "green washing," marketing without consideration for the impact it provides to the cause.

What is your definition of a social entrepreneur?
A Social Entrepreneur is someone who applies their skills, knowledge and innovative ideas towards creating social impact first versus maximizing profits. Our business model strives to help organizations be better, smarter marketers and maximize their available resources. We help organizations with their digital marketing because we feel it can be highly leveraged.

What do you feel are the absolute basics that must be in place before a nonprofit can successfully fundraise for a cause?
Whether it's a digital[37] appeal, an event or direct mail campaign, either online or offline, nonprofits must be willing to invest in

38

marketing dollars associated with fundraising success. To launch a digital campaign in market, there must be a very thoughtful and well-orchestrated strategy that includes a strong website presence, a broad base of online followers and a differentiated mission.

Have you found that an 80-20 rule applies to online fundraising?

Online fundraising breaks the 80-20 rule! It presents a way for organizations to diversify their fundraising portfolios and reach a younger donor. The younger donor might not give a large amount initially but if a nonprofit can capture a gift, it will be possible to develop a value stream over time. The nonprofit's ability to reach this audience is much more scalable, too, since only so many large donors exist. Online donations can make an organization's giving ratio 50-50 while adding balance to the revenue stream.

How do online and offline fundraising work together?

Multi-channel communication cultivates a higher and more sustained donor relationship. Although organizations are starting to test how a direct mail campaign might impact an e-mail solicitation effort, it's only possible to assess multichannel outreach with good data. Nonprofits must take a "hard look" approach at their data to understand how best to communicate with their audience, what offer to create and through which channels.

How does Giveo maximize the opportunities associated with various new technologies, including social media?

Our proposition is "Why would you message somebody who is twenty five, no kids and not married the same way you might communicate with a fifty year old, married and with children in college?" Giveo analyzes a nonprofit's "house file" of emails and creates profiles and market segments. Then, we determine the specific offers, content and channels best suited to each segment, measuring conversion rates as well. It's important to speak relevantly to each donor segment.

Know Your Donors

In a recent study conducted by the market research company, Hope Consulting, and consisting of an online survey of 4,000 individuals, it made the following recommendations for nonprofits to improve their fundraising capabilities:

- Segment on behaviors, not demographics.
- Tag and track your donors by segment.
- Determine what segments are best for your organization.
- Develop consistent outbound marketing that appeals to target segments.
- Prioritize investments based on what will drive donor behavior.
- Capture donors early.
- Understand how to manage different segments when approached.

Source: "Money for Good: The US Market for Impact Investments and Charitable Gifts from Individual Donors and Investors" May 2010

What do you feel is key to donor relationships?
A good cadence of communication creates loyalty. Content should be clever, creative and not always about soliciting a donation.

Technology provides transparency and generates loyalty. Donors want an organization to clearly demonstrate how money has been spent. After a campaign has ended, if an organization repeatedly communicates, thanks the donor for the gift, demonstrates it's impact, maybe with a video or e-mail, and promises to "keep in touch," a supporter will notice! Furthermore, such strong communication might motivate the donor to post the great news and results to a Facebook wall, providing additional benefit.

Can you give me an example of a campaign that focused mainly on engagement versus fundraising?
The Brooklyn Community Foundation conducted a crowd sourcing contest. The contest asked for nominations of individuals who were

40

"doing good" across five different categories, areas that reflected the foundation's work. There was a nominating campaign, followed by a voting period. The winner was recognized at a community event. For many, the crowd sourcing contest was the first time they had ever engaged with the Brooklyn Community Foundation. Instead of over-soliciting potential supporters, the contest engaged them in a non-threatening, fun way while showcasing the foundation's work.

The campaign had 300,000 votes and 300 nominees. If you engage 20,000 of those participants (or 6%) in a future campaign and convert slightly less than 10%, it might possibly translate to 2,800 new donors. Even if most gifts are between $20-$50, a future campaign, based on analytics from the previous crowd sourcing contest, might add significantly to the Brooklyn Community Foundation's bottom line.

How can you raise money most effectively online?
The most effective campaigns know their target audience and have specific content in the fundraising appeal. An optimized website segments the donor and creates different "landing" pages. Imagine having ten to fifteen pages with optimized content? By speaking directly to the donor, the intention is to achieve higher conversion rates.

Through digital tracking, it's possible to segment even further. For example, suppose a donor with household income of X and buyer segments of A,B,C is also an active Facebook user and a "Big Influencer." Our campaign will prompt this supporter and perhaps even offer an incentive, to share the information with the several hundred *friends*[38] in her network, creating new links to potential donors.

Are there business disciplines that should be incorporated into fundraising?
Thoughtful strategy, a content editorial calendar and marketing tactics need to be incorporated into any online campaign, whether it's for engagement, fundraising or awareness. A measuring framework is also important and might answer questions such as: Who engaged with the platform? How many supporters donated and when? Were donations made while "pushing" the Facebook page?

Did Twitter impact donations? How did the e-mail campaign affect results?

When an organization employs the business discipline of analyzing and tracking results, it's possible to better maximize resources associated with marketing efforts, as well as use the data to build future campaigns.

How do you feel corporations should support philanthropy?
Corporations should leverage their assets to build capacity into a nonprofit. Once a company has identified a "cause partner," one well matched with its brand, it should look inside the nonprofit for the opportunity to help instead of only "writing a check;" a company might assist with marketing or website design, for example. It's also incumbent on nonprofits to identify opportunities for maximizing the corporate partner relationship. Often nonprofits care only about the check!

What role should government play in supporting nonprofits?
Government should continue to provide financial support but not play a role on the programming side. Generally government programmatic support is accompanied by additional demands and or constraints, preventing a nonprofit from doing its most effective work.

What do you know now as a leader that you wish you had known sooner?
I have come to appreciate the relationship, people-side of the business, whether it's with employees or on the constituent level. How do you motivate people to do the hard work? What is the proper incentive structure for employees to go "the extra mile" and even give the organization "shower time?" "Shower time" is when an employee is so motivated that they have crisp moments of problem solving during "off-hours."

Has there been anything that has helped you get the "shower time?"
People want to be listened to and valued; the empathy element of business. Empathy crosses an organization as a unified thread both in how to engage and communicate with employees, customers and partners. How do you listen and empower within the construct of

achieving measureable objectives? Many internal issues are just "people issues," and the need for better alignment on where and why the organization is moving in a particular direction.

How do you feel nonprofits might move to a new level of resilience and sustainability in the future?
I see nonprofits already moving to a new level of sustainability. There's an ambitious and smart demographic graduating from college that has grown up in a new world, one with information at their fingertips, extensive transparency and a demand for relevance. This generation wants to make an impact and earn money.

There's a great opportunity for nonprofits to engage and attract this group through a hybrid, quasi-nonprofit and for-profit model. Boards need to change their own composition, too, and invest in digital technology, more progressive employees, and whatever else is associated in being more modern.

Where would you rather work?

Answer: At nonprofits that leverage progressive technology to affect the organization's future success.

"Imagine starting at a company that (1) doesn't have much of a website and offers a dial-up Internet solution or (2) issues a MAC Book on the first day, utilizes broadband and has a big social media presence." Which would you chose? (Ed Messman, Giveo)

Discoveries

- Modern means investing in digital technology, attracting ambitious and smart college graduates, with a hybrid nonprofit/for profit model and a progressive environment for employees and boards.
- Cause marketing must organically relate to the nonprofit and its mission.
- Online marketing offers enormous leverage.
- With the ability to reach a broader audience, online marketing breaks the reliance on traditional giving ratios, while also attracting younger donors.

- Donor segmentation and customized communication are no long optional...no longer a luxury, but rather a necessity.

What discoveries did you get from reading Ed's interview? Share them with our other readers at: www.FundraisingInnovators.com

Key Take Aways

Below are actionable steps you can apply to your own organization. Put these on your calendar, share them with your team, and assign the necessary resources. Add these to your annual plan, follow up and measure your results to completion. Ideas mean little until acted upon!

- Create digital marketing campaigns built on strong analytics; what are the questions in your campaigns used to measure results?
- Guided by the discipline of analyzing and tracking data, multi-channel communication cultivates a higher and more sustained donor relationship. Segment and personalize your marketing strategies.
- A good cadence of communication creates loyalty, especially for thanking a donor and demonstrating the impact of their donations. Create and manage a communication calendar.
- For-profit corporations should leverage their assets to build capacity into a nonprofit. If you're a business, identify what skills and knowledge you might bring to a nonprofit. If you're a nonprofit, what areas of expertise need to be bolstered? What business might offer help?
- Do you highlight the unique attributes of your organization in a progressive or exciting message?

What else do you plan to do as a result of ideas from Ed's interview?

Robert Wolfe: Crowd Sourcing and Modern Internet Practices

"Whether it's feeling passion, winning a prize, having fun, and then telling all your friends about it, self-interest drives fundraising success."

- Robert Wolfe, co-Founder, Crowdrise

Themes
Technology, Crowd Sourcing, Peer-to-Peer Fundraising, Online Corporate Collaboration, Online Marketing, Self- Interest

Profile
Type: Fundraising Site
Location: Detroit, MI

Mission: "Crowdrise is about giving back, raising tons of money for charity and having the most fun in the world while doing it. Crowdrise is way more fun than anything else aside from being all nervous about trying to kiss a girl for the first time and her not saying something like 'you've got to be kidding me.'"

Background

Crowdrise, a popular online fundraising site, is downright fun and, co-Founder Robert Wolfe is even more engaging. Using humor throughout the website, Crowdrise offers an easy and most compelling online experience. Maintenance fees are charged on donations "To make sure (they) don't go out of business trying to help everyone raise lots of money for charities." The Crowdrise response for those that object to fundraising: "If you don't give back, no one will like you."

Clear marketing directions are provided for every step of a campaign on Crowdrise and with added retail-like incentives, everyone wins. There is even, a Crowdrise Featured Human Person, (CFHP) in addition to entries solicited for the "super-sought-after Crowdrise napkin badge!"

What's innovative? Crowd Sourcing and Self-Interest

Through the use of social media, Crowdrise empowers the individual to fundraise for a cause and appeals to those that communicate almost exclusively online, especially younger donors. This iPhone generation has less patience for the long newsletter. Instead, Crowdrise embraces "Crowd Sourcing." Spreading the word to "friends" not only matters for raising money but also has now become a standard practice for building and engaging community. Crowdrise pioneered the individual fundraising page that mimics and maximizes a Facebook-like experience.

Crowdrise understands self-interest. Self-interest drives individual success. Donors (your customers) want to know WIIFM (What's In It For Me). Nonprofits, business owners, and social entrepreneurs would benefit from understanding this self-interest paradigm. Crowdrise provides a modern platform for fundraisers and donors alike to impact a cause that they "care deeply about."

Interview

What community does your organization serve? Who are the benefactors?

We serve lots and lots of people, especially those who are fundraising and the many charities that benefit from their work.

What brought you into this particular organization?

My brother and I owned *Moosejaw*, an online, outdoor sports company. Our business approach was "nonsensical" meaning not too serious and tons of fun.

In 2007, after selling the majority share of our business, we shifted gears and started to develop concepts for online fundraising. While researching the philanthropic space, we discovered that not only were centralized resources scarce, but there was little fun and engaging around online fundraising. An opportunity, thus, presented itself: we might apply the same game mechanics from our retail experiences at Moosejaw to creatively engage people, in online fundraising.

We asked our friend, the producer, Shauna Robertson, if she could help us and she in turn asked her friend, Edward Norton for help. Norton was training for the NYC Marathon to raise money for the Masaii Wilderness Conservation Trust. He offered to let us help him with his fundraiser. His campaign became a collaboration case study for the tools created on Crowdrise.

How do you differentiate your organization from other businesses?
We differentiate ourselves by offering a platform that proactively engages our donors with retail-like practices, offering prizes to participants and an incentive point system. We give participants reasons to be self-interested in their success. Our solution is more modern than other online opportunities and does so much more than just skim the surface in fundraising.

What do you mean by modern?
Our website tools are clearly well beyond Web 2.0[39] and offer more of a groundswell approach. This capacity to build growth is unique in the online space. On our site, we offer a Crowdrise "Your Charitable Life" page that reflects someone's Facebook-like testimony about philanthropy. While Facebook defines your friends and Twitter highlights what is happening to you now, the Crowdrise "Your Charitable Life" page lets the participant say to the world: "Here is how I give back." No one else provides this unique platform.

What are the absolute basics that must be in place before someone can successfully fundraise for a cause?
First, the cause must be tangible, something that meets an easy to understand, big impact need, for example, selling malaria nets for $10.

Second, successful fundraising needs passion and/or reach. When raising $20,000, imagine ten, very enthusiastic people raising $2000 each or, as an alternative, 2,000 people donating $10 each, attaining the same fundraising goal with a much smaller donation. One or the other scenario is necessary.

Third, the fundraising message must be notable. In other words, what's compelling about the cause? What will people notice? No one will attain reach without participants having an audience for their broadcast. That is an absolute basic. While it's important to know how to tell your story, as noted above, it's essential to tell your story to as many people as possible.

What is uncommon about fundraising with Crowdrise?

If you're relentless and follow the Crowdrise model, it's now possible to raise money from your couch – versus attending a dinner event or going to a party. Look at the millions of shoes sold by Zappos online. Fifteen years ago, no one thought consumers would abandon the bricks and mortar retail experience. The paradigm has shifted in fundraising, too. (See related story on Zappos and Online Fundraising in Appendix)

Does the 80-20 rule apply to fundraising? In other words, do 80% of your gifts come from 20% of your donors?

I don't have data to know whether an 80/20 rule applies online at Crowdrise. I do believe the power of a crowd is meaningful. Think about American Idol: decisions are made by a mass collaboration of the audience. The same scenario might occur between a fundraiser marketing a cause on Crowdrise and the donor looking to support a cause. If someone wants to raise $1,000 on Crowdrise, I'm guessing that, most likely, forty people would give $25 or one-hundred people would give $10. We just do not have enough online data yet to determine an actual giving ratio.

Are there business practices that should be incorporated into fundraising? Why or why not?

Crowdrise combines social networking, crowd sourcing and online retail tools, reflecting a modern business approach. Recently, Moosejaw received a $5000 gift from Patagonia to give to charity. Moosejaw reached out to its customers and proposed the following: "Customers, nominate your top charities. Then, Moosejaw will select the top ten charities from your responses. The top charities will have two weeks to raise $10,000. Whichever charity raises the most money will receive the $5000 from Patagonia."

The results? Consumers nominated over 500 charities and the Moosejaw/Patagonia campaign raised $40,988 ($30,000 more than

48

anticipated). More than a thousand people donated. The winner, Yellow Dog Watershed Preserve raised over $12,000 and then received an additional $5,000, bringing the total to $17,000. The second and third place teams, the Mississippi Valley Conservancy and the Michigan Land Use Institute raised $9,570 and $8,771 and although they did not win the $5k, they retained all the money raised because of their efforts.

In the past, a check represented a corporate gift donated, a nice gesture. With this campaign, we raised 800% more money and provided insane exposure for the corporate partners, Moosejaw and Patagonia.

How might corporations support philanthropy?
The Moosejaw and Patagonia example illustrate how corporations might embrace philanthropy and leverage donations through crowd sourcing and social media, making it fun and cool, embracing the modern campaign elements of the Internet. Instead of just writing a check, companies realize the upsides for everyone: Crowdrise raises money for charity, customers become involved, individual charities benefit and the whole fundraiser reflects well on the corporate sponsor. Raise money based not on the charity that the corporation likes best, but focus instead on what pleases their customers.

How have social media and technology changed fundraising?
The change is so dramatic it's like working on a type-writer instead of a computer or sitting by a landline phone versus bringing your cell phone wherever you go. You have more tools now, than ever before, to be an effective fundraiser.

What does the online versus offline marketing model look like?
The online and offline models embrace the real world and the internet at the same time. Think about how it feels to watch a charity's video at an event. You're probably thinking, "I need to do everything possible for this organization," yet the organization does not send you an email that night nor the next day asking, "Thank you so much for coming and donating $25. Now we want you to raise $250." Crowdrise was built for engineering events and follow-up. On Crowdrise you can easily direct your donors to take additional action.

Is there anything else you'd like to share?

The most effective campaigns create self-interest on behalf of the individual fundraisers. Whether it's feeling passion, winning a prize, having fun, and then telling all their friends about it, self-interest drives success. Organizations must help fundraisers and donors feel proud of their achievements. It's not called the "you-phone" but the "iPhone," right? For the iPhone generation, fast and simple communication that announces intention is key. People like to share what they are doing with their friends and feel good about it. This is not derogatory, just modern.

The Plan for the Moosejaw/Patagonia Campaign

- Moosejaw sends one dedicated message to its email list telling their customers that $5k is available to a charity.
- Moosejaw customers nominate their favorite charities to potentially win the $5k.
- Moosejaw and Patagonia choose a total of 9 charities from all of the submissions.
- The 9 charities populate a Moosejaw/Patagonia custom branded page on Crowdrise.
- Moosejaw sends a follow-up email to its list letting customers know the final nine charities competing for the $5k.
- Crowdrise contacts the 9 organizations and the charities unleash hell trying to raise the most money possible.
- Whichever organization, among the 9 charities, raises the most money from their supporters in two weeks will win the $5k.

Source: Crowdrise Case Study report, June 2011

Discoveries

- The change in technology is dramatic. There are more tools now than ever before to be an effective fundraiser.
- Social media is a perfect vehicle for promoting someone's efforts. Friends like to tell their friends about what they care about.

- Young donors are weary of events or long newsletters. They desire fast and simple communication, especially utilizing social media.
- The power of a crowd is meaningful. It's now easier to mobilize people to give online, creating mass collaboration similar to the American Idol model.
- Embracing the modern campaign elements of the Internet, businesses can align fundraising efforts with their customers' desires.

Key Take Aways

- Self-interest drives individual fundraising success. Identify peer-to-peer fundraising opportunities in your organization.
- Reach and passion are necessary for success. It's essential to tell your story to as many people as possible.
- What part of your marketing and outreach efforts target the younger donor?

Chapter Two - Integrate Marketing: How To Differentiate Your Organization Today

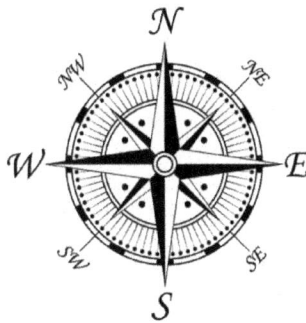

Although essential, a clearly articulated mission does not by itself translate into an effective marketing message:

"It's not enough that a nonprofit's work represents something meaningful. Nonprofits need to be marketers and effective storytellers. They must clearly define a brand story, especially within their specific category. A strong and consistent message will deliver results from precious marketing dollars and provide clarity for potential donors as to why they should invest in a cause." (Simon Mainwaring)

Further, successful marketing requires a commitment to a plan and an accompanying budget:

"Whether it's a digital appeal, an event or direct mail campaign, either online or offline, nonprofits must be willing to invest in marketing dollars associated with fundraising success. To launch a digital campaign in market, there must be a very thoughtful and well-orchestrated strategy that includes a strong website presence, a broad base of online followers and a differentiated mission." (Ed Messman)

A study published in March, 2010, "The Next Generation of American Giving," revealed that almost all generations will donate across multiple channels.[40] Consistent communication across multiple marketing channels is crucial to nonprofit marketing today. But how might integrated marketing be achieved?

In the following interviews, Katya Andresen, Rich Rainaldi and Steve Daigneault demonstrate how integrated marketing can differentiate your organization from others. This involves understanding what makes your organization unique and how to communicate it. These marketing professionals will also address the importance of defining you audience by segment with messages relevant to each demographic.

Look also for valuable insights into the use of analytics and measurement tools. In addition to programmatic impact, strong analytics are at the core of executing successful marketing campaigns tied to clear objectives.

Katya Andresen: Online Marketing, Donor Loyalty and Gratitude

"It's not about you; it's about your audience."

-Katya Andresen, COO of Network for Good

Themes
Online Marketing, Donor Recognition and Loyalty, Behavioral Economics, Gratitude, Financial Sustainability

Profile
Type: Technology-based nonprofit, Internet charitable giving platform
Established: 2001, "to turn technology into a force for good."
Founders: AOL, Yahoo and Cisco
Location: Bethesda, MD and San Francisco, CA
# of Employees: 37
Budget: $12M
Money Raised (2009): $120 million, total amount of money raised to date:
- Over $500 million in online donations to more than 60,000 different nonprofits.
- Returned $25 to the sector for every $1 invested in Network for Good.
- "Taken fundraising viral and raised well over $3.4 million via fundraising widgets[41]."

55

Mission: "Network for Good is a dynamic, technology-based internet-nonprofit…that leverages social entrepreneurship and business acumen to meet the ever-growing philanthropic needs of individuals, companies and nonprofit organizations. Network for Good envisions a world where generosity is unleashed, with opportunities to give back at every person's fingertips. To achieve this vision, Network for Good empowers nonprofits and partners with the platform, marketplace and know-how to scale generosity and advance good causes."

Network for Good serves the following communities: consumers, nonprofits and companies. It offers the following services:

- Fundraising tools: Helps nonprofits raise money on their own websites and on social networks with free and low-cost fundraising tools.
- Online donations: Enables giving to any charity registered in the US (more than one million) at www.networkforgood.org, through fundraising widgets on social networks, and via partners' websites.
- Corporations: Powers cause marketing campaigns and giving for partners such as Capital One, J&J and Clinique.
- Research and Volunteerism: Users can research any charity and search from among more than 40,000 volunteer opportunities. Individuals can also search for volunteer opportunities through a state Volunteer Network sites: California, Louisiana and New York.
- Star power: Links people with celebrity philanthropists including Kevin Bacon, Ellen DeGeneres, Robert Duvall, Colin Firth, Ricky Gervais, Joaquim Phoenix, and the 'Six Degrees.org' initiative.

Background

Although Katya describes herself as "profoundly impatient to do good," I noticed her thoughtful and deliberate style during our interview. Before working with Network for Good, Katya worked as Senior Vice President of the Sutton Group, a marketing firm that supports the nonprofit, government and foundation arenas. She also worked abroad for CARE International as well as being a marketing consultant for a diverse group of international clients. Prior to working in the nonprofit sector, she was a foreign correspondent for Reuters News and Television in Asia, and for the Associated Press, the *San Francisco Chronicle* and *The Dallas Morning News* in Africa. She has worked at Network for Good for six years as the Chief Strategy Officer, being hired after interviewing their management for her own book, *Robin Hood Marketing*. *Robin Hood Marketing* "steals" from corporate cause marketing campaigns and defines ten essential rules for communicating an organization's message.

Throughout our interview, Katya displayed her social marketing savvy regarding the use of technology, fundraising and best practices for nonprofit management. She defined social marketing as the use of for-profit ideas influencing behavioral change. Katya fortified her answers with facts from multiple research studies.

Interview

What are the core principles of marketing?
The essence of marketing is to understand the world from the perspective, of the audience we're trying to reach, then using that knowledge to craft an effective strategy to engage those constituents. Although a nonprofit believes its cause is just, information about the mission alone will not motivate people to act. Instead, marketing must demonstrate why a cause is relevant to the values of potential supporters.

Which organizations do the best job differentiating themselves in their marketing and why?
Nonprofits that are good at marketing focus on results; identifying an action they want people to take to achieve a clear social good outcome, then planning backwards into an outreach strategy. I have seen a very small local organization, A Wider Circle, as well as a more well-known national nonprofit, DonorsChoose, practice this principle effectively.

A Wider Circle, an organization that helps families who are just getting onto their feet in their own homes, tells amazing stories through individual emails. A typical email from the Executive Director starts with words from a recipient: "I just want to thank you. Tonight, for the first time I saw my son sleeping in a bed and I was so excited I kept getting out of my own new bed and running to his room and watching him sleep." As a donor, I felt fundamentally moved and motivated to continue my support. While A Wider Circle does not have a fancy website, its emails tell stories that provide a very clear sense of what I as a donor can do, and what will happen when I act. There's really no excuse for all organizations not to tell their own stories well.

At DonorsChoose, I have the opportunity to connect with a specific classroom. I see pictures of the children, hear from the teacher and am engaged with the classroom's needs in a very personal way. I know exactly how my money will be spent, the lives I'm touching and the impact my donation will make on the children. DonorsChoose creates a level of personalization that is tangible, compelling and accessible to all nonprofits.

Have you seen any successful collaboration between nonprofits sharing a similar mission?
The most effective collaboration between nonprofits is created when the following question is answered: "Who wins when we win?" In other words, identify organizations that share the desire to make a certain change occur and build a coalition around that shared vision. A good partnership is created when there is a clearly shared agenda around specific actions.

My favorite example is the Theodore Roosevelt Conservation Partnership, a motley crew of unlikely bedfellows. This group includes hunters, land conservation groups, and outdoor sports enthusiasts such as members of Trout Unlimited and the Union Sportsman Alliance. These groups come together because they recognize mutual benefit from wetlands preservation.

As exemplified by the National Organization of Rare Diseases, collaboration can also create a stronger voice. This group of "orphan diseases" has increased research funding and become more powerful and effective by working together.

What are the absolute basics that must be in place before any organization can successfully fundraise online for a cause?

The first, most basic requirement is a solid marketing strategy that focuses on connecting with people, regardless of shiny technology tools and objects. Technology will not save an organization if it lacks strong online relationships.

The second requirement is a mastery of the most basic aspect of an online presence; your organization's website. Sixty to eighty percent of donors will visit an organization's website before making a donation of any kind or writing and mailing a check.

As a litmus test for forging connections on the website, I propose your organization answer four sets of questions:

1. Why me? As a donor, why should I care about your cause? How is it personally relevant to me?
2. What for? What happens if I make a gift? What specific need will be met?
3. Why now? What is the urgency around making a donation at this time?
4. Who says? As trust erodes in our official voices and canned messages, voices beyond our own become critical. What credible authority figure or third party supports this cause?

Additionally, websites need a big "Donate!" button that connects to a simple checkout page and maintains an emotional connection.

The third basic is effective email to attract donors to your site. Most money is raised online, either from your site or an email solicitation. Once those two pieces are in place, it's worth exploring an investment of time in social media. Social media should be approached as a means to build relationships with supporters over time. Only after strong relationship building has occurred might successful fundraising through social media be possible.

How does online fundraising intersect with offline fundraising?
If I could wave a magic wand, I'd like to solve one problem with online outreach; the lack of integration between different channels such as online technology, direct mail, the Major Donor department, and even telemarketing. Donors actually switch between channels. There are not online and offline donors but rather individuals who respond in different ways. Effective campaigns integrate the

approach across channels, playing to the same theme and Ask, recognizing the multiple ways a donor might respond.

Do you have a sense that there is an 80-20 rule that applies to online fundraising?

Year after year, three quarters of all charitable giving in the United States comes from individuals. In other words, 75% of $290.89 billion dollars is donated annually by individuals.[42] This shocks people but it's really important to remember from a fundraising perspective. Although large donors represent a big segment of that individual piece, it would be a terrible mistake to only solicit major gifts from a few people. For some organizations, the same amount of money can be raised from many donors making smaller donations. A typical organization needs both. If a nonprofit does a solid job of soliciting and cultivating the smaller donors, over time their emotional investment in the organization will grow and possibly translate into bigger gifts in the future.

Is this relative to the online piece? Do you feel that the large donors are coming online?

Through website donations, the average gift online is three or four times the average gift offline. The average gift online is over $100, while offline, it is under $30.

The number of large gifts online is growing and, in fact, as documented in the research paper, "The Wired Wealthy[43]," there are already a significant number of big online donations, defined as $5,000 or more.

Are there business disciplines that should be incorporated into fundraising? Why or why not?

Marketing matters, of course, but behavioral economics is also extremely applicable to fundraising and is often overlooked. Behavioral economics teaches that consumers are predictably irrational when making buying decisions. Consumers pay more attention to emotion than facts. This is highly relevant to fundraising. Individuals make donations based on how personally connected they feel to a cause. In addition, individuals pay attention to social norms versus market factors and examine what others are doing before making a buying decision. Thus, a fundraising thermometer can be effective. Behavioral economics is full of lessons for fundraisers.

What do you feel is the key to loyal online donor relationships?
It's very simple: gratitude, helping donors feel in touch with the difference they have made, over and over again. Research shows that when people donate, doing something good for someone else, it releases endorphins into the brain and creates real happiness.

Unfortunately, nonprofits have a customer service problem; the number one reason people stop supporting a nonprofit is because of the way they are treated by the charity. More often nonprofits treat supporters like an ATM machine, mailing the next envelope or calling during dinner, or neglecting existing donors. Instead, nonprofits need to stay connected to the personal and emotional reasons for a gift and provide meaningful stories, repeatedly, on the impact someone's donation makes.

How do you feel it's possible to express gratitude online?
Technology is uniquely suited to deepen human relationships over time. Watching a video, we can see more vividly the impact of a donation. We can listen to and experience an interview with individuals who are benefitting from a gift. Sending thoughtful, inspiring emails that cost less than pennies can build the relationship with a donor. Emails and other uses of technology, if grounded in human experience, can both express gratitude and also create sustained loyalty over time.

How have technology and social media changed fundraising, and how might organizations maximize opportunities associated with these technologies?
Everyone on this planet is inherently generous. The job of a fundraiser is to ask people to give in an inspiring way, unlocking that charitable instinct. Technology provides more opportunities to make The Ask[44] more compelling.

According to Julien Smith and Chris Brogan, authors of *Trust Agents*, social media is a place for people and ideas, not corporations or nonprofits. It's a platform for personal expression and, in fact, we as marketers and fundraisers are not in charge of the message anymore. To me, the promise of social media is the peer networks and the idea of friends fundraising and sharing their passion for a cause. This is a big shift for organizations and not every nonprofit is structured, nimble nor open-minded enough to participate in this change.

What do you think about crowd sourcing?
Friends asking friends for money, like at Crowdrise, is one use of crowd sourcing, focused on money. But, this is only one piece of social media. Social media is about joining conversations that already exist and reaching out to community, versus waiting for others to find your organization or page. It's about locating people who have a natural affinity for your cause and understanding where they congregate, and how to listen and facilitate conversation.

How might corporations support philanthropy?
I see a shift in how corporations view philanthropy. Six years ago, when I first started at Network for Good, I worked off to the side with corporate philanthropy departments. Now, we partner with the Marketing Department. Corporate philanthropy has become an integral part of driving a company's bottom line while benefitting others, creating a halo effect for the brand and indirectly motivating employees. It's nice to have good happen in the world as a result of cause marketing.

How might nonprofits move to a new level of self-reliance?
Network for Good is a strong case study in becoming self-reliant. Initially we were dependent on the founding corporations for funding. Today, we are 100% self-sustaining, generating enough revenue ourselves to cover operating and capital expenditures.

Nonprofits should find ways to create revenue while advancing their mission. Network for Good generates something of value to different partners willing to pay for those services. We provide low cost online outreach services for nonprofits as well as a cause-marketing platform for corporations. Since the funding environment can be uncertain, it's especially important to have revenue sources that provide stability when donations have decreased.

Do you consider Network for Good a social enterprise[45] and a nonprofit? Where is the distinction?

Our organization has the soul of a charity but the mind of a business. Although we exist for our mission, we want to be self-sustaining. We promote a very results-oriented culture with dashboards and thermometers that constantly measure our results versus our goals. If Network for Good raises less money with technology than we did a year before, then we are failing in our work. At the end of the day, it's about human lives, not just shareholder value, so we have to be very demanding of ourselves.

I wish more nonprofits approached their work with the same focus on clear results.

Katya Andresen- An Inspired Leader

"I am profoundly impatient. I spent seven years living in developing countries, and the poverty and tragedy I saw on a daily basis left me with an acute sense of how important it is not just to help people, but to do it really well and really quickly. The child in Cambodia or the cyclone victim in Madagascar doesn't have time for us to wordsmith our mission statements or waste time with lackluster fundraising efforts. We have a moral obligation to be extremely efficient and effective at what we do, right this minute. What gets me motivated and energized is to help well-intentioned people to do that every day, through innovative marketing. I strive to do this at Network for Good, where I work, and I sure tried to do it in my book as well.

In addition to being impatient to do good, I am impatient to find the next great shoe, the latest post on every single celebrity-obsessed blog and the secret to being the uber-mom who makes perfect cupcakes for the class Halloween party instead of rushing to Giant bakery department at 10 pm the night before. My greatest joys are my two extraordinary young daughters and one extraordinary economist."

Source: Biography, Katya Andresen, Amazon

What do you know as a leader that you wish you had known sooner?

From the moment of graduating from college, I wish I had understood that it's important to demonstrate why what you're doing matters to others. In marketing, it's not enough to tell someone the value of your cause. Rather, you must connect your cause to a donor's existing values. Relationship building and proving personal relevance are continual exercises in fundraising.

Secondly, fundraising is the business of happiness. It's not the practice of extracting money. Fundraising provides an opportunity for people to make an amazing change in the world through their gifts. The emotional ROI is far above any retail therapy. We can be far more successful when we ground our work from a place of abundance versus simply focusing on our own need.

Discoveries

- Donors switch between different channels and/or individuals respond to solicitations in different ways.
- Behavioral economics[46], the study of "buying" decisions, holds lessons for the fundraiser: consumers and donors alike make buying/donating decisions based on emotion. In the case of a donor, gifts occur because of a strong personal connection to a cause, also reinforced by friends and peers making the same decisions. Marketing must first and always demonstrate why a cause is relevant to the values of potential supporters.
- Social media should be considered as a third marketing leg after website and e-mail strategy. A compelling well-organized Website and effective e-mail marketing should be well established before engaging in social media.
- Corporations have shifted their perspectives and view philanthropy more and more as an integral part of driving the bottom line.
- Collaborations build on a shared vision that successfully answers the question: "Who wins when we win?"

Key Take Aways

- Identify an action for supporters to take for achieving a clear social good outcome. Then, plan backwards into an outreach strategy;
    - Why should I care about your cause?
    - What specific need will be met if I donate?
    - What is the urgency of making a donation at this time?
    - What credible third party supports this cause?

- The key to loyal donor relationships is gratitude, helping donors feel in touch with the difference they have made, again and again. How have you thanked your donors?
- Everyone on this earth is inherently generous. The fundraiser's job is to ask people to give in an inspiring way, unlocking charitable instinct. What about your cause unlocks inherent generosity?
- Identify ways your nonprofit might create revenue while advancing mission.

Rich Rainaldi: How Metrics Tell a Story

"Analytical tools should primarily assess how an organization can deliver a better program or service and not over-emphasize donor acquisition. Isn't it more important to use metrics to arrive closer to solutions?"

-Rich Rainaldi, Co-Founder and Principal, CiviCore

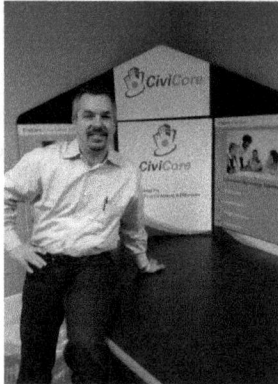

Themes
Technology, Marketing, Metrics, Donor Loyalty, Transparency, Board Management, Leadership, Behavioral Economics.

Profile
Established: 2000
Location: Denver
Number of Employees: 15
Customers: 400 Customers in 42 states and 4 countries
Current Philanthropic Work: Board Member and past Chair, Colorado I have a Dream Foundation; Board Member, Denver Public Schools Foundation; Board Member, Planned Parenthood of the Rocky Mountains

Past Philanthropic Work: Past Chair, Urban Peak; Past Board Member, Summer Scholars. In addition, Rich has served on the board of over a dozen nonprofit organizations in Colorado and across the country including Rebuilding Together USA. He is the recipient of the Minoru Yasui Award for Community Service and, in

2008, received the William Funk Community Builder Award from the Colorado Nonprofit Association.

Business: Customized software platforms and "Technology for People Making a Difference"

Clients: CiviCore has in-depth knowledge of organizations working in the following categories: Nonprofits, Government Agencies, Foundations, and Evaluators. Their primary customers are "at risk" youth-serving agencies. A second customer segment is with organizations that manage individuals and teams of volunteers, especially within the environmental stewardship sector. A third client group includes a mix of different nonprofits involved with improving and rebuilding housing and or food bank management. CiviCore also works with foundations and knowledge management systems, in addition to victim service organizations.

Services: All services are customized. They include technology platforms for Client Relationship Management, Community Information, Evaluation Management, Giving, Mentor Management, and Volunteer Management.

Mission: CiviCore's mission is to make a social impact at the local, national and international level through our work with our clients. To achieve this mission our focus is on improving the use of information within the social sector[47]. We accomplish this by: (1) developing information solutions for clients within social sector industry; (2) consulting with social sector organizations regarding information problems.

Background

During the 2010 Christmas season Denver was abuzz with the successful results of the first "Colorado Gives Day." Over $8 million was raised for Colorado nonprofits through the Giving First website. In 2011 donations totaled over 12 million. CiviCore created this outstanding platform!

The system processed as much as six donations per second with thousands of donations processed during the day. Online giving is just one example of CiviCore's huge impact on a nonprofit's work. CiviCore's customized technology platforms, whether for tracking clients, volunteer or community indicators, generate useful metrics for telling a nonprofit's story.

Rainaldi feels that metrics, one or two key indicators, should be used as a management tool for refining program performance. Similar to a successful company that strives to offer an improved service or product, nonprofits should also continually strive to better their programmatic results.

The over emphasis on too many metrics can be unrealistic for many nonprofits that balance manpower and resources. Yes, analytics are important, says Rainaldi, but to a certain extent, donors are engaged because they believe in the organization's mission. Donors will give to a nonprofit that demonstrates positive client and program outcomes. Money will follow success.

Well-run nonprofits have business practices built into their operations asserts Rainaldi. Most wrong doings in the nonprofit industry are often overblown. In fact, with clear internal controls and transparent practices, nonprofits are often more accountable than many companies.

In his interview, Rainaldi's viewpoints are straightforward and extremely useful, with particular focus on metrics and business operations. His answers clearly demonstrate his breadth of expertise, knowledge and passion to contribute to the greater good.

Interview

What are the absolute basics that need to be in place before an organization can fundraise?
Nonprofits need strong stewardship with accounting systems that internally process and track donations and are separate from the board structure and its oversight. To engender the public's trust, nonprofits must complete the 990[48], conduct an outside audit and be transparent on how donations are received and spent. I'd also report on accomplishments, especially successful changes amongst clients.

Second, nonprofits need to have a clear sense of mission and connect it to potential donors, including those outside their friends and family circle. Like seeking venture capital, as nonprofits grow, they must tell their stories to sophisticated "investors."

68

Do you consider CiviCore a social entrepreneurship?
CiviCore has a social mission: we serve nonprofits, public agencies and foundations. We strive to act like an accounting firm, a trusted partner, deeply understanding our nonprofit's business. While customization of software solutions defines a big part of our services, we consult on how to accurately and easily collect data that creates a compelling nonprofit story. While we provide a top service at a fair price to the social sector, we still must make a profit.

All Board Members are Fundraisers Asserts Rainaldi

In addition to a nonprofit's Executive Director, all board members must fundraise, all the time. One group solicits new donors, a second asks past donors for more money, and the third writes the Thank You(s). Thoughtfully recognizing a donor is as important as asking for a donation.

What are the business practices that should be incorporated into nonprofit management and fundraising?
There is often a perception that the nonprofit sector does not have strong internal controls and processes similar to a business. But, in fact, they do. Frankly, nonprofits have a higher level of accounting principles and structure because of tax code requirements and the need to satisfy the public trust. Often any malfeasance is exaggerated relative to the size of the industry. We have 400 CiviCore customers and not one has ever experienced collapse because of improper practices.

Nonprofits must have a strong board to provide checks and balances as relates to the Executive Director and Staff. The board is responsible for financial oversight and might need to make difficult decisions. In terms of operating like a business, the board determines that monies are well allocated on systems, employee compensation and programs. Often there are different pressures on how to spend nonprofit resources relative to the mission, even choosing to end the year with a negative cash flow or cross-subsidize programs.

From the start, nonprofits are almost always under-capitalized. They are trying to "do the right thing" but with one hand tied behind their

69

back. Less money is invested in infrastructure and, in the long run, this can hurt them sometimes.

What is the key to loyal donor relationships?

First, nonprofits that thank you the best are the organizations that you connect with for a longer period. Second, nonprofits engender loyalty when they connect a Major Donor's passion to a specific proposal which not only matches the nonprofit's need but, more importantly, makes the connection obvious to the supporter. Third is the Thank You. Follow up and recognition programs must be in place. It costs zero money for a board member to call a Major Donor or write a personal note. Without a thoughtful thank-you, donors will go elsewhere.

Please tell me about the value of metrics for a nonprofit? What should be measured and why?

Community Indicators

It's important to think first about the level of metrics you're assessing. Around the country, conversations have focused on measureable community indicators of success. In rural Colorado, for example, indicators might be improved high school graduation rates and a decrease in drunken driving incidents. Nonprofits might want to connect their efforts to the bigger, community indicators. These broader measurements attract donors.

Analytics and Donors

Our current desire to hold nonprofits accountable for pre and post researched-based outcomes can strain resources. Although there is a growing and smaller donor segment that demands specific metrics, the majority of supporters donate because they buy into a nonprofit's mission. The nonprofit's work speaks for itself.

Analytical tools should primarily assess how an organization can deliver a better program or service and not over-emphasize donor acquisition. Isn't it more important to use metrics to arrive closer to solutions? Both types of measurements are important but programs with strong results will attract donors anyway.

Donors will support a nonprofit that communicates well, has a clear mission and cultivates trust, whether through a friend's referral or standard transparent practice. Money follows those metrics that let donors digest certain chunks of program success.

Analytics That Gauge Improvement
It's healthy for every organization to have metrics which are their "fly-wheel to success[49]," one or two indicators at the core of their mission, that measure improvement and are clearly reportable back to the community. There needs to be defined milestones along the way for achieving the ultimate goals.

Successful organizations build the analytics into their processes from the start. Look at the Summer Scholars program in Denver. Started in 1993, it evaluated success by testing students, at the outset and end of the program. Although measuring success was initially done as pro bono work, it eventually became built into the budget.

Analytics can be used as a management tool. During a typical year, the Summer Scholars program conducts a pre and post-measurement and then, in the fall, intently studies the data. In this case, key indicators were on reading improvement and attendance. Measurements allowed the Summer Scholars reading program to identify areas for improvement and adapt its teacher ratio and curriculum for the following year. Program results have steadily improved year over year because of this consistent evaluation.

Metrics Can Be Difficult to Define
Donors, please take note…while summer reading is easier to quantify, sometimes measurements are not as straight-forward. At Urban Peak, a homeless shelter for youth, a 50% success rate means that youth have experienced stable housing for two years. If a girl is in the shelter, she is not prostituting herself on the street corner. How do you measure the intangible benefits of Hector staying off the streets while still struggling with his drug-addiction? A tension between tangible and less quantifiable measurements exists at the heart of a nonprofit's work. While some impact is easy to measure, like school engagement, it can be difficult to determine the best indicators for success, especially if it's about saving a life.

Metrics From the Start For Better Management of Client Data and Tracking

Instead of waiting for organizational growth and the accompanying increased complication of the data, I'd like to see all organizations, especially "Starts Ups," commit to collecting more demographic information from the beginning. Basic demographic data is valuable. Just as customer data is tracked by companies, to know who is coming through the door, what customers look like and how to respond, it is equally important for the nonprofit to understand clients. Even basic demographic information allows the nonprofit to ask questions and be better managers. Urban Peak, for example, saw an increase in girls involved in the sex trade. Because of the data, counselors were better able to provide the right services and partner with other organizations for these clients. Data painted a clearer and more current picture of their client's profile.

What motivates people to donate to a cause?

Donations often occur because someone, a trusted friend, asks another, to support a cause. Giving also happens because of a personal connection. Churches, for example, still receive the largest amount of charitable donations because people have an emotional and relational connection to these communities[50]. Often past experiences can create outreach towards a cause. People, who have survived cancer, for example, gravitate to nonprofits focused on a cure. Sometimes, all it takes for motivating a donor, is a nonprofit's mission, representing something that a person truly cares about, like love of a household dog or cat and the passionate loyalty to the Humane Society.

Is there anything you know now as a leader that you wish you had known sooner?

Successful nonprofit leaders are "Super-Connectors," as referenced in *The Tipping Point* by Malcolm Gladwell; people who mentor, collaborate, inspire, give back, speak at panels, raise their hand and show up!

A Stanford study published in the "Stanford Social Innovation Review," came to the same conclusion: "...real social change happens when organizations go outside their own walls and find

72

creative ways to enlist the help of others." According to authors, Crutchfield and McLeod, high-impact nonprofits engage individuals and organizations outside their sphere to achieve results not possible on their own.[51]

When an opportunity presents itself, often these "Connectors" and their "High-Impact" nonprofits, regardless of size, will be at the table.

The Definition of a "Connector"

- "Connectors know lots of people. They are the kinds of people who know everyone;

- They manage to occupy many different worlds and subcultures and niches;

- Their ability to span many different worlds is a function of something intrinsic to their personality, some combination of curiosity, self-confidence, sociability, and energy;

- By having a foot in so many different worlds, they have the effect of bringing them all together."

(page 38, 46, 49,51; *The Tipping Point*, Malcom Gladwell, 2000, Back Bay Books, Little, Brown & Company)

The Influence of Non-Profit Information on a Donor
According to a study conducted by Hope Consulting in 2010, the majority of donors, regardless of their demographic, spent little time researching a nonprofit before they donated. When donors did conduct research, they looked for simple facts and figures, information that was easy to understand.

The top three types of information sought out by donors was:

- A nonprofit's overhead ratio;
- The "amount of good" accomplished by the nonprofit;
- How charitable donations were utilized.

The report found that all donors, regardless of type, felt the most important reason for giving was a deep care for the cause.

Rainaldi reminds us to watch out for an overemphasis on meeting donor demands for metrics versus authentically measuring the most important key indicators. If metrics illustrate the difference the nonprofit is making in accomplishing its mission, donors will be supportive. The Hope Consulting report reinforces this view.

("Money for Good; The US Market for impact Investments and Charitable Gifts from Individual Donors and Investors;" May, 2010; Hope Consulting, www.hopeconsulting.us; Funded by the Metanoia Fund, the Aspen Institute of Development Entrepreneurs, the Rockefeller foundation, and the William and Flora Hewlett Foundation.)

"The Flywheel Concept Defined[52]"

"Picture a huge, heavy flywheel – a massive metal disk mounted horizontally on an axle, about 30 feet in diameter, 2 feet thick, and weighing about 5,000 pounds. Now imagine that your task is to get the flywheel rotating... Pushing with great effort, you get the flywheel to inch forward, moving almost imperceptibly at first... You keep pushing, and the flywheel begins to move a bit faster, and with continued great effort, you move it around a second, rotation... Seven eight...fifty...a hundred...you keep pushing... Then, at some point, breakthrough! The momentum of the thing kicks in your favor... Your pushing no harder than during the first rotation, but the flywheel goes faster and faster... What was the one big push that caused this thing to go so fast? Was it the first...the fifth...the hundredth push? No! It was all of them added together in an overall accumulation of effort applied in a consistent direction..." According to Jim Collins, sustained effort, "step by step" and "decision by decision," creates transformation of a company from Good to Great. The same can occur for nonprofits who routinely measure, year after year, the effectiveness of their programs and client outcomes. According to Rainaldi, sustained effort to measure results will ultimately allow a nonprofit to come closer to achieving its mission.

74

Discoveries

- A strong board provides checks and balances for the Executive Director and staff of a nonprofit. All board members should be raising money all the time.
- Analytic tools should be used as a way to manage and measure program outcomes. There are a variety of analytics to consider such as: community indicators, donor support, program improvement, and client impact and tracking.
- Nonprofits have a higher level of accounting principles and structure because of tax code requirements and the need to satisfy the public trust, often more than many for-profit companies.
- Nonprofits that are the best at thanking donors often retain their supporters for a longer period of time.
- Leaders and nonprofits need to be "Super-Connectors." High impact nonprofits look outside their own walls for resources and to further their mission.

Key Take Aways

- Fundraising success can arc off of consistent and positive programmatic outcomes which allow a nonprofit to tell its story. What key metrics tell your nonprofit's story and success?
- Establish clear metrics from the start of a program. Nonprofits who routinely measure their effectiveness over time will come closer to achieving their mission.
- Without a thoughtful thank-you, donors will go elsewhere. How thoughtful is your recognition program? What is memorable about your Thank You?
- Engage others outside of your nonprofit to accomplish your mission. Who are the "Super Connectors" on your board and or staff?

Steve Daigneault: Authenticity and Storytelling

"Messages white-washed by committee aren't what inspire people to act."

-Steve Daigneault, Senior Vice President, M+R Strategic Services, Washington, DC

Themes
Advocacy, Storytelling, Online Engagement, Transparency

Profile
Type: Nonprofit Consultant

Location: Headquarters, D.C.

Other Locations: New York City, New England, Missoula, MT and Portland, OR

Number of employees: 90 staff with an online team of roughly 35, the largest department within the agency

Mission: "...to deliver highly tailored campaign strategy and services to leading nonprofits working on behalf of the public interest. Our teams specialize in campaign planning and execution, online advocacy, online fundraising, government affairs, communications, field organizing, and activist training. We integrate these advocacy tools within a single firm, providing our clients with a pioneering approach to 'full service' campaign planning and management."

Background

Steve has over 15 years of experience as a grassroots organizer, communications specialist and online strategist. Before coming to M+R, he served as the Managing Director for Internet Communications at Amnesty International USA, where he developed an email strategy that nearly tripled Amnesty's list in less than three years. He launched award-winning campaign micro-sites and helped grow Amnesty's online fundraising program, even in the midst of the September 2008 stock market crash. Steve has also been a consultant and strategist for the U.S. Holocaust Museum, Aspen Institute, Audubon Society, SaveOurEnvironment.org, Opportunity Agenda, and United Nations Association.

In 2009 Steve joined M+R Strategic Services and has managed clients including PBS, the American Cancer Society, and the U.S. Fund for UNICEF. An activist at heart, he enjoys working at M+R because it focuses on "progressive" nonprofits, those politically left of center. He not only understands the connection between advocacy and fundraising represented by two forms of nonprofits, the 501c3 and the 501c4, but also draws upon sharp online marketing savvy for the benefit of his clients.

Daigneault recommends that nonprofits maximize news events with timely "Call to Action" e-mails, website promotion and social media dialog. He suggests that social media creates huge opportunities for employees, at all levels of an organization, to engage constituents. It's crucial that marketing efforts reflect an individual's values around a cause using meaningful stories.

Interview

How are advocacy and fundraising tied together?
Advocacy and fundraising are similar in the sense that both represent action aimed at making positive changes. Typically, advocacy means influencing decision-makers on behalf of an issue on local, state and federal levels, in the legislatures, corporations or other organizations in our society. Actions might include sending letters, e-mails, in-person visits, and phone calls. Compared to advocacy, fundraising uses donations to move an issue forward.

M+R Strategic Services works with both 501c3 and 501c4 organizations. Differences between these two types of nonprofits are reflected in how strictly the IRS audits revenues and disbursements. Lobbying activities are highly restricted for a 501c3 but monies are completely tax-exempt. A 501c4 does pay taxes and, therefore, is allowed to lobby. Since the mission of a 501c4 aims to achieve a certain change and/or improve a cause, like a 501c3, it is still considered a charity.

Which nonprofits do the best job of differentiating their cause by marketing?

Organizations differentiate themselves when they take risks and have a distinct message, one not created "by committee." Messages should feel like they originate from an empowered individual, who speaks with personality, on behalf of the organization. Avoid too much cautious jargon from policy experts. Although policy experts communicate in a complex and nuanced way, that kind of messaging does not typically resonate with the broader public.

Started in 2006, with a list of two hundred thousand names, Avaaz, a "Move On"[53] type of global nonprofit, maximizes the creativity of individuals. About fifteen individuals from around the world, who work from their homes, have grown the database to over eight million members in less than five years. Basically these individuals create and manage campaigns without anyone editing their stories. Leading up to the Beijing Olympics, Avaaz created "The Olympic Handshake Campaign" that encouraged peace, friendship and dialog with the Chinese government over human rights abuses in Tibet. The Handshake Campaign started with the Dalai Lama, went to the streets of London and then moved online. The campaign travelled the globe and culminated with the British Prime Minister delivering Avaaz's global petition with 1.67 million signatures to the Chinese embassy. Avaaz created a campaign that fostered participation by the average person. Similarly, nonprofit marketing campaigns need to reflect individual values for a cause.

Author's note: According its website, Avaaz represents "a global web movement to bring people-powered politics to decision-making everywhere."

Have you seen successful collaboration between nonprofits sharing a similar mission?

I have witnessed collaboration through the use of "chaperoned"[54] messaging. For example, Amnesty International and UNICEF, organizations working in the same general sphere of work, might send out an e-mail that includes a petition or campaign from the partner organization. When a supporter signs the petition on behalf of the partner organization, this might translate to a potential new donor. This type of partnership benefits both organizations and helps each organization broaden their online communities.[55]

What are the basics that must be in place before any organization can successfully fundraise for a cause?
First, there must be a problem that grips people emotionally. Then, the organization must offer a clear solution to the problem.

What are the most successful fundraising vehicles?
For health and medical research organizations, online Personal Tribute/Memorial Pages[56] work well, in addition to some type of event, like a walk benefitting cancer research. People usually have a personal connection to the cause, making these vehicles effective for fundraising.

A second way to raise money online is a "Call to Action" response to news event. Successful advocacy groups quickly mobilize messaging around an issue to leverage current outrage and raise funds. Timing is extremely important, as is access to a large e-mail list. This type of fundraising occurs primarily via e-mail and is supported with web promotions and social media spaces.

Are there business disciplines that should be incorporated into fundraising? Why or why not?
In many ways, fundraising departments within a nonprofit work like for-profit companies; they rigorously track their efforts against forecasts and projections. Campaign units that are trying to create change in the world often don't have similar metrics to assess their performance, and many times this leads to a lack of rigor or discipline.

I often think that nonprofits could learn from the corporate world about decision-making. Many nonprofits over-value the input of every staff member, which leads to ineffective decision-making. There's a fine line between soliciting input from the appropriate people, versus providing every individual with veto power, allowing them to hijack a project. Nonprofits need to clearly identify who has the responsibility to finalize decisions and leaders need to be willing to push back when decisions continue to be repeatedly questioned.

What do you believe is key to loyal donor relationships, especially online?

Although I don't have data to substantiate this assertion, my sense is that it's easier to cultivate loyalty online than it is offline. An organization can send more messages for less money online, which also creates the ability to experiment with tone and authenticity. Ultimately, a message that feels highly relevant, authentic and personal creates loyalty.

Transparency also plays a huge role in building donor loyalty. Donors ask, "What did my donation impact? Where did my money go?" Frequent and thoughtful online "updates" foster better relationships with donors. Inviting donors in, offering them a seat at the table, and showing them the details of what's really happening inside your organization and on the projects donors are supporting fosters loyalty and excitement.

How has technology and social media changed fundraising?

Online fundraising is all about the moment, what's happening right now, this very minute. Being timely and relevant has always mattered in fundraising, but technology and the pace at which we receive news and interact with each other makes how we talk about this very moment that much more important. With that said, you still need an emotional problem and solution.

Social media allows an opportunity for the nonprofit to engage in conversations about what the public and supporters want to talk about. Organizations that stay open and invest time in online conversation through social media interaction with supporters will build brand and loyalty. Social media is not easy to measure, but that doesn't lessen its importance.

How should organizations maximize the opportunities associated with technology whether it's email, Facebook or their website?

Nonprofits need be comfortable with allowing appointed staff to speak with constituents the same way staff would speak with their friends. Social media is about human beings interacting with each other, people who have feelings, personalities, strengths and weaknesses. White-washed[57] communication doesn't work in this environment.

I saw a presentation at the Nonprofit Technology Conference in 2010 where the American Red Cross social media team spoke about its evolution. It was fascinating that such a large, well-respected brand, one that has many "police," allowed relatively young staff members to speak directly to the public. The American Red Cross team talked about a mistake they had made, and how responding like normal people worked well with their followers. This is in such contrast to a corporate and or bureaucratic process and infrastructure that might normally issue press releases.

How might corporations support philanthropy?

Matches! Even though some people believe that donation matches are passé, we've tested these recently and they absolutely work. Matching donations are probably the single best tactic you can use when running an online fundraising campaign.

Do you have a mantra that you use yourself when working with others or volunteers?

Trust your gut and be willing to take risks. Being too cautious might have saved me from making mistakes, but it also might have kept me from achieving some really important victories. My most valuable skills and strategies came from making mistakes. Moving forward, I learned something essential.

How might nonprofits move to a new level of resilience and self reliance?

Increased transparency would help nonprofits change and make hard decisions. More transparency might force nonprofits to fire people who are underperforming. Or, it would encourage the elimination of ineffective programs that exist because a few people have a vested interest.

In fundraising, specific appeals that need money at a certain place and time out-raise unrestricted campaigns one hundred-fold. Although nonprofits need unrestricted monies for the bottom line budget, they should stay open to "earmarked"[58] campaigns. It might make more sense to attract new supporters by letting them select the program they want to support.

Is there anything else that you'd like to share?

Overall, I think nonprofits are too cautious. It's rare that you see a nonprofit with a strong, distinct personality. Those organizations that let their passion through, take risks, and speak to the public and to their supporters with open, personal language are often the ones who succeed most at raising money.

I don't think nonprofits expose enough of their work to the public. Donors only hear about inadequacies after a reporter uncovers some type of scandal. This hurts all organizations. Instead, nonprofits need to address publicly what is not working and how they plan to improve and move forward.

Messages white-washed by committee aren't what inspire people to act. It's better to take a clear stance, when it matters, than to send a perfect but totally safe message after the moment passes.

Discoveries

- With messaging that feels highly relevant, authentic and personal, it's easier to create loyalty online than offline.
- Online marketing allows nonprofits to share the impact of a donor's gift with consistency and repetition.
- Online fundraising is all about the moment, what is happening right now around an emotional problem and solution. Being timely and relevant matters.
- Nonprofits don't examine their own weaknesses nor expose enough of their work to the public which harms the entire sector.
- Nonprofits need a clear decision making structure to move actions forward.

Key Take Aways

- For online collaboration "Chaperoned" messaging works well; a nonprofit sends a petition or campaign e-mail on behalf of a partner organization. Who might your nonprofit partner with for a "Chaperoned" message?
- Maximize news events with timely e-mails that have a "Call to Action," such as "Donate Now."
- To build brand and loyalty, allow your employees to engage with constituents through social media. How does social

media complement your marketing programs? Who in your organization utilizes social media and how is it organized?

- If mistakes are made, act human and respond (versus issuing an impersonal press release). What is your social media policy and action steps for responding to a negative comment or event?
- Corporate matching programs work! Does your nonprofit use these? How might you improve them? How do you recognize employees that contribute through corporate Matching Programs?
- Be willing to examine challenges and face them "head on." What kind of review is in place for evaluating core programs?

Chapter Three – Champion Corporate Philanthropy & Collaboration

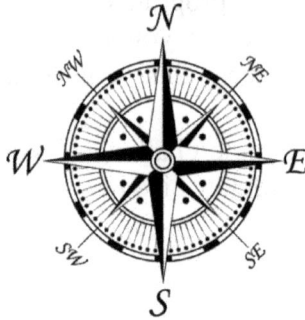

Corporate philanthropy has been embedded in our culture for decades. In 2010, corporate donations increased by over 8.8%, representing 5% of total giving or $15.29 billion. This amount included $4.70 billion donated in grants from corporate foundations. In the prior year, 2009, corporations increased donations by 11.8%. The increase for two years was 21.6%![59]

Unfortunately current perceptions of Wall Street greed and corporate over-indulgence, reinforce a different story, almost negating this sector's generous contributions. As gleaned from the interviews, however, there is tremendous opportunity today to expand corporate relationships. Interviewees contend that more and more companies recognize the benefit of charitable giving to not only the bottom line but for their employees and community as well.

Everyone likes cash! The same applies to the single-minded nonprofit focus on procuring the corporate check. Although corporate underwriting is crucial, as demonstrated by the past donation numbers, we'll see in the following interviews, that corporate philanthropy has much broader potential, from employee engagement programs and collaborative cause marketing campaigns to capacity building strategies. The nonprofit & corporate relationship requires education on both sides of the equation and a commitment to long-term relationships.

In today's funding environment, there are many different partnerships between nonprofits, corporations, foundations and government agencies intersecting at the point of "doing good." It's not always easy to work with other organizations, especially when collaborative goals feel intrusive, threatening an organization's sense of self-determination. Collaboration, however, is an essential ingredient for maximizing resources and accomplishing a nonprofit's mission. It can inspire innovation, allowing for more creativity and mind share towards finding a solution. In addition, a united voice often has more power to influence others.

Interviewees, Richard Crespin, Simon Mainwaring and Ryan Scott show us how to cultivate sustainable corporate opportunities. Francisco Gonima and Peter Wilderotter provide insight into how to structure successful collaborations.

Richard Crespin: Philanthropy and Corporate Responsibility[60]

"Corporate Responsibility reflects how a company delivers its goods and services with the minimum negative and the maximum positive impact."

-Richard Crespin, President , *Corporate Responsibility (CR) Magazine*, Founder and Owner of SharedXpertise

Themes
Corporate Giving, Corporate Responsibility, Shared Values, Nonprofit Management, Capacity Building, Business Strategy

Profile
Type: Corporate
Number of Employees: 15
Founded: 2001
Mission: (Shared Xpertise, owner of *CR Magazine*) "To provide senior executives with unparalleled learning, meeting, and networking experiences on corporate responsibility, human resources and financial management."

Background

Richard Crespin founded a market research firm called SharedXpertise. As the business grew, he acquired *Business Ethics Magazine* in 2007 and re-named it *Corporate Responsibility (CR) Magazine* in 2010. SharedXpertise also publishes *HRO Today* (Human Resources Outsourcing) and organizes the COMMIT!Forum and HRO Today Forums, which are annual conferences in Corporate Responsibility and Human Resources respectively. Richard Crespin serves as Executive Director of the

Corporate Responsibility Officers Association and Global Executive Director of the Human Resources Outsourcing Association.

Every year, *CR Magazine* publishes a "100 Best Corporate Citizens" list with philanthropy as one of seven factors defining a strong corporate citizen. Few, if any, organizations have ranked corporate responsibility for as long as *CR Magazine*. According to a recent blog from the *CR Magazine* website, the "100 Best Corporate Citizens" list "rewards transparency and accountability" and reflects a "relative ranking" since companies are compared with their peers year over year. Companies on the "100 Best" list are part of the Russell 1000[61] composite, the largest publicly traded multi-national firms in the United States.

The annual COMMIT!Forum is the single largest gathering of leaders improving business and society through Corporate Responsibility practices. Reflected in the 2011 theme for COMMIT!Forum, "Good Business Makes the Difference," Crespin believes that "good corporate citizenship and good business go hand in hand."

CR drives the commitment of good business making the difference and helps Russell 1000 companies work with their state core stakeholders, including their employees, investors, communities, governments, and non-government organizations to create solutions to some of society's toughest issues. As described in his interview, corporate philanthropy aligned with revenue goals provides tremendous collaborative opportunities for nonprofits.

Interview

What personally brought you to CR Magazine?
I have always had a passion for public policy that drives solutions to some of the world's most daunting challenges. I believe that the corporation, as an entity, has the most impact on people's lives. Most people work for, live next to, invest in, derive their wealth from and or purchase goods and services from corporations. Therefore, the best way to create positive change in the world is by working with corporations to improve the way they impact society.

How do you define corporate responsibility (CR)?

In the broadest sense, CR reflects how a company delivers its good and services with the minimum negative and the maximum positive impact. We measure and evaluate CR across seven different categories: financial performance, employee relations, human rights, environmental impact, climate change impact, corporate philanthropy and governance.

What role does philanthropy play in CR?
Philanthropy is one factor in how companies create impact, positive or negative. Particularly in the United States, corporate philanthropy plays an important role in society. Our tax code encourages companies to establish foundations in order to act philanthropically. We also have a social contract within the fabric of our communities that recognizes the need for charitable activities and includes funding causes not supported by government. Companies fulfill these needs.

How is Philanthropy valued in relation to the other factors in your assessment?
Although philanthropy is the second lowest in weighting, it is still an important factor. We have reduced the rating over time because we do not want company's to engage purely in "Checkbook Philanthropy"[62] simply writing checks unconnected to strategy. At the turn of the century wealthy individuals, the Robber Barons, exemplified a "Pillage and Repent" cycle of giving; doing whatever was necessary to be successful in business and then "buying their way into heaven" later. We want to discourage this type of behavior.

Consider as well the classic Milton Friedman[63] approach to corporate philanthropy; companies maximize profits, return dividends to the investors and leave philanthropy to the individual. Instead, we want companies to engage in philanthropic activities that build on their core and long-term business strategy. We want them to act systematically and think sustainably from the beginning versus "repenting" later in their corporate life.

How do you feel about a movement that espouses a 5% annual donation of a corporation's profits should be donated to charity?

Tithing-like requests or a flat percentage feel like a tax. I'm not as concerned as much with a percentage as much as I am with results. Philanthropic activity needs to fulfill business strategy.

Do you feel there's an 80-20 rule that applies to Corporate Responsibility?
Yes and no because everyone has the opportunity to make an impact in different ways. We focus on the Russell 1000 companies because they employ 70-80% of the American workforce and represent 92% of our publicly traded firms in the United States of America. A small change made by these companies will reverberate around the world.

How do you feel business should support philanthropy?
First, companies need to examine their long-term goals. According to Michael Hopkins and Martin Reeves, in an article recently published in the Sloan Management Review, one benefit of corporate responsibility program is a company's ability to build capacity in a new innovative way, where none existed before. IBM for example uses its corporate philanthropy to not only "do good" but to also open new markets and provide services in places that normally cannot afford to do so.[64]

Using philanthropy for the benefit of reputation either builds your brand or mitigates a negative feeling, depending upon the life cycle of the company. The Fair Trade Movement was created in response to the perception that large multi-national corporations were taking advantage of indigenous farmers and producers, as in the coffee industry. Starbucks engaged in "fair trade" as a way to burnish their brand and create a positive association, perhaps even eliminate any past guilt. On the other hand, a new coffee retailer might decide from the beginning to deliberately participate in fair trade, establishing a philanthropic approach from the beginning.[65]

How do you believe nonprofits can create loyal relationships with corporations?
Over the last few years, as private and government funding has decreased, I've received many calls from NGO's[66] (non-governmental agencies) about how to make an "ask" that will engender a positive and consistent response from the corporation. NGO's and nonprofits should study a company's strategy and create an "ask" that speaks into it. Demonstrate to the corporation that the

company benefits as much as their contributions help the cause. Look for product-placement based donations that provide future economic opportunity. Write the commercial that illustrates in three years, for example, how the company created impact and a positive brand: such as, "Did you know that Hewlett Packard's power computers were used in the Afghan elections?"

In what ways have companies helped nonprofits raise money as well as collaborate?
Although volunteer hours are unrecognized and, thus, limited and discouraged by our tax code, one of the most powerful ways to engage a leading company is to ask them to lend the time of their employees. A consulting firm or other "white collar" firm, as in the financial or technology sector, have great knowledge workers[67] with skills that would benefit the nonprofit.

Other ways to collaborate might include an event that allows a company to showcase its products and/or a corporate matching program. Both permit employees to donate their time, money and organizational skills.

What do traditional corporations and social entrepreneurial businesses have in common?
Corporations have inherently fulfilled a social good throughout the grand scope of their history. That's why they exist; to create the clothes we wear, the drinks we consume and the television shows we watch. Over the last twenty to thirty years, however, businesses developed a maniacal focus on shareholder value and profits. This singular goal generated odd behaviors and undesirable results, including the Great Recession, financial crises and our current economic struggles. Recently, in response, we've seen a great rise in consciousness that has fueled the development of social entrepreneurs; those that are simply socially responsible in their day jobs. Over time, social entrepreneurship will become just part of the way people conduct business.

How does technology and social media affect corporate responsibility?
Technology and social media have had a profound impact. Social media provides almost instantaneous feedback, adding pressure on transparency. Not too long ago, Nestle made some unfortunate

remarks on its Facebook page that caused a deluge of messages from Green Peace, a left-of-center German political party and, ultimately, led to product and sourcing changes.

Social media has also produced a democratizing element in communication and new opportunity for fundraising. For the first time in human history, anyone, anywhere, with an Internet connection, can send a message that potentially can be read by everyone else, who is connected. If charged with raising money for a NGO or nonprofit, I would study the 2008 Obama Campaign as well as current fundraising for political candidates[68]. I would also investigate Indonesia and other places around the world where messaging and reach have greatly influenced actions and increased financial contributions (Please see information on Avaaz in Steve Daignealut's interview as an example of grassroots advocacy).

How might corporations help nonprofits move to a new level of self-reliance?
Nonprofits suffer from the same problems as a small business in two core areas. First, the business founder, like a baker for example, tends to be extremely passionate about the work, baking, but does not necessarily understand the skills needed to maintain the business, keep the lights, power and heat on, so to speak. Nonprofit leaders suffer from the same lack of education despite passion around a cause. Very few universities offer nonprofit business education in our country. Companies can provide capacity with people that know business, like accountants, HR employees and sales people. In many ways, fundraising is selling. Companies can help nonprofits by lending knowledge and transferring it to them.

Is there anything that you know now as a leader that you wish you had known sooner?
Although this might sound "hippie-dippie" or even Buddhist, and I'm the furthest from that you can be, people who "pursue their joy" are making a real difference in the world. Many instead worry only about how to do their jobs and or chase after the dollar. I have found that the more I focus on "my joy," the more success I have.

A second mantra is to "hire slowly, fire quickly." Recruit and retain the right people. If, however, an employee is not a good fit, make changes for not only the organization's good but the employee as well.

Is there anything else that you would like to share?
CR Magazine has studied the Russell 1000 companies for over ten years. We have noticed that the top twenty-five percent improve their corporate responsibility year over year. As a group, differences between them are becoming much smaller. Yet, the remaining seventy-five percent of the Russell 1000 "pack" is "stuck." They feel unsure how to act and answer the call when approached by a NGO and nonprofit.

Nonprofits and companies must find common cause. We need business leaders who understand social issues and are willing to risk engagement in conversations. We want nonprofits that understand corporate priorities. Our annual COMMIT!Forum last November, 2011, encouraged "commitment conversations" in which successful partnerships shared their results and taught others how to engage.

Discoveries

- A benefit of CR programs is a company's ability to build capacity in new innovative ways within a nonprofit.
- Corporate philanthropy needs to integrate with the business strategy. Start with a company's long term goals to identify fit.
- Using philanthropy for the benefit of reputation either builds your brand or mitigates a negative feeling, depending upon the life cycle of the company.
- The US tax code encourages companies to create foundations and act philanthropically.
- Seventy-five percent of the Russell 1000 companies feel unsure how to answer the call when approached by a nonprofit.
- A rise in consciousness about "giving back" has accompanied an increase in social entrepreneurships in society. Overtime, social entrepreneurship might become a standard way of conducting business.

Key Take Aways

- When supporting a nonprofit, companies should focus on their core and long-term business plan versus writing a check unconnected to strategy.
- Nonprofits should study a company's strategy and create an "Ask" that demonstrates how a business benefits in addition to the social impact of their contributions.
- One of the best ways to engage a company is to ask them to lend the time of their employees, "knowledge workers," such as accountants, HR employees and Sales and Marketing. What areas does your nonprofit need help with? What companies might be able to fill this need to mutual benefit?
- Hire slowly, fire quickly. Recruit and retain the right people.

Simon Mainwaring: Shared Interest in Building Community and Relationships

"If we can collaborate, cooperate and be creative together, in new ways never imagined, it will inspire others to do the same and, suddenly, we will have brand consumer partnerships and large communities, irrespective of time, geographic or language barriers, that will cooperate and exist, around fundamental values critical to being human. Technology is teaching us to be human again."

-Simon Mainwaring, Author and Social Entrepreneur, *We First*

Themes
Social Media, Technology, Cause Marketing, Corporate Philanthropy, Brand Marketing, Corporate Responsibility, Self-Interest

Profile
Type: Social Branding Consultancy
Location: Santa Monica, CA
We First, (the book) published June 2011

Clients: Over the past nine years, We First has worked with a variety of "Client Partners" including ad agencies, direct clients, digital

94

companies, production companies, purpose-driven companies. An extensive list can be found on the We First website.

Awards: Multiple awards from organizations such as Cannes Advertising Festival, One Show, British Design & Art Direction, Communication Arts, Kelly Award, AICP Winner, Clio, London International, Andy and AWARD (Australia)

Mission: "We First is a social branding consultancy that helps brands, nonprofits and consumers use social media to build communities, profits and positive impact."

Background

Simon Mainwaring has had good fortune; he has a law degree, a successful career in advertising working in Australia and London and during the last twelve years, in the United States. Yet, even after big success, his life felt unfulfilled. "Exactly what am I doing again?" he asked. Simon missed the opportunity to say good-bye to his father before he died, introducing the need to be mindful of the finite time on earth. Further, with the birth of his children, Simon contemplated the type of world that he would leave behind when he was gone.

A speech presented by Bill Gates at the 2008 World Economic Forum in Davos, Switzerland acted as an additional catalyst for Mainwaring to find his purpose. Gates asserted that government and philanthropy alone could not fix the current crisis. The private sector needed to play a larger role. This proposition resonated with Simon. His skill set and extensive experience with global brands aligned with the need for the private sector to make a bigger impact. Three and a half years later, his book, *We First*, contributed to the conversation.

Simon Mainwaring calls for a fundamental shift in how business conducts itself. He wants corporations to derive profits from sustainable practices that align with causes and build community by inherently "doing good." Mainwaring is gutsy in demanding a change to the underlying motivations of capitalism.

In his interview Simon presents huge opportunities in the use of social media across all sectors. Social media will fuel improved engagement with the donor community, transparency and a better use of marketing resources. He also advocates collaboration, representing a shift from "Me First" to "We First" thinking.

What promise does this hold for the nonprofit? Shifts in how corporations view their global role will facilitate broader collaboration with nonprofits, ultimately accelerating solutions for the worlds' problems. Nonprofits can also no longer sit on the sidelines when it comes to utilizing technology, which is finally accessible and affordable.

Interview

What community does We First serve?
The *We First* concept serves multiple communities. The first and largest is the global community. We live in an intimately connected and mutually dependent global community. We can now communicate through social platforms with people on the other side of the world.

Second, *We First* refers to employers and their employees; the community at work. On the third level are the relationships of a brand and its customer base, requiring shared interest of both parties. As a broad concept, *We First* encompasses the various hats we wear as stakeholders in life; parents, employees, CEO's, shareholders, or as global leaders.

How do you define Corporate Responsibility?
The term, Corporate Responsibility, is odd, almost a misnomer. The label presumes that it only exists outside the normal workings of a business. Instead, Corporate Responsibility should be the realization and expression of a brand's core values that not only pays attention to the bottom line but also does something meaningful for its customer community. Corporate responsibility is actually innate; a core essential of being a company rather than something for "window dressing" or marketing strategy.

Existing corporate philanthropy does not provide enough donations and, in a bad economy, contributions will decrease. Despite large profits, companies have escaped being responsible for their impact on society, the environment and employee base. They have been held only accountable for fiduciary results.

The separation between "Living" and "Giving," the practice of "corporate profits, first" and then, "give back," must end. It's costing us the very sustainability of society and the middle class, a brand's customer base.

What role does philanthropy play in corporate responsibility?
When a brand reaches out to a philanthropic organization, one consistent with its core values, it can be an incredibly powerful partnership. The brand gains access to a new community while enlisting its resources in service of the cause. Too often cause marketing is not aligned with the company's values. Not only is the public relations value of "doing good work" lost, but disingenuous behavior is doubly dangerous and alienates the customer who, especially since the revelations of 2008, is particularly distrustful.

Are Consumers Distrustful?

The Trust Barometer Index measures trust in business, government, NGO's and media. According to the Edelman's 2011 "trust barometer" report, trust in U.S. business was only five points above Russia! Explanations for this drop include, "prolonged fighting between business and government; sustained unemployment rates...the U.S. as an epicenter of multiple crises in 2010, such as the oil spill and SEC investigations."

Authenticity and transparency are particularly important to the consumer: "57% of consumers will believe negative information about a company they do not trust after hearing it just once or twice. When a company is trusted, however, only 25% will believe news about it after hearing the news once or twice." (Adelman's Report 2011)

This issue is not just a perception but will affect the bottom line results for a company. Similarly, a nonprofit that builds a strong foundation with its donors will engender long-term loyalty.

How might corporations support nonprofits? What might it look like?

My approach is slightly counter-intuitive. Although alignment of a company's core values with a nonprofit makes sense, a far more effective solution is the systematic integration of cause into a brand's for-profit business model. Like servicing a car every two years, companies need to build "giving" into the very act of business. Here's why: (1) it will improve society at large and ultimately the sustainability of a company; (2) it will build a community of customers around shared values and successfully drive bottom line profits.

Is this strategy the concept of "Contributory Consumption[69]?

As a way of ending the false separation between "Living" and "Giving," Contributory Consumption is a simple idea that a small portion of every product's sale is allocated to a cause in alignment with a brand's core values. This extends to retail, mobile, credit card, online and virtual goods transactions. If only 5% of the full profit sector donated $.01 on the dollar, the results would still dwarf the $14 billion raised annually by corporate foundations. This is a systematic and sustainable solution because purpose is integrated into the for-profit model and resources are built in consistently through active consumption, in good times and bad.

What is the Global Brand Initiative (GBI) and what might make it successful?

The Global Brand Initiative is the coalescence of corporate resources into a formal association, to advance social change. Our survival instinct and crises of sufficient magnitude are forcing competitive brands to work together to solve problems bigger than their own self-interest.

There are already indicators that changes in how we conduct business are occurring: such as   Patagonia's Sustainable Apparel Coalition[70], now representing 30% of the global apparel market; First Lady Michelle Obama's "Let's Move"[71] initiative in which a group of companies represent 25% of the US food supply are working together to fight obesity; and Nike's "Green Exchange"[72] through which companies share intellectual property to address climate change.

98

Authors Note: Additional examples of businesses collaborating for a greater good include Product Red[73], Socialvest[74], and Architecture for Humanity.[75]

Although the GBI utilizes Contributory Consumption to generate funds, it would also leverage the skills sets of the private sector around the world, including management, training, research, development and "bricks and mortar" infrastructure. There's also an opportunity for brands to bring their skill sets to bear on long term infrastructure solutions to emergency crises, like the Haitian earthquake. This way the GBI framework benefits those in trouble on the ground, employee volunteers, a business' profits and society at large.

Why do you think those collaborations have been successful and what might nonprofits learn from these partnerships?
Collaboration brings together unrelated people, allows for greater creativity, infuses new energy into a process, spurs pooled resources and inspires solutions outside the confines of one person's work place or mindset. Within the nonprofit sector there's understandable competition for mind share, fundraising resources and share of voice in a cause conversation. Although the market place is very competitive, organizations can resolve issues much more quickly and effectively by working together.

How do you define social entrepreneurship and how is We First an example of social entrepreneurship?
We First is an expression of social entrepreneurship because it views business, life, our interactions and technology through the lens of the collective whether it's represented by the global community, your city, state or family.

In the long term, our own self-interest is best served by serving others. Social entrepreneurs understand an expanded definition of self-interest to include themselves and the others, the seven billion other people on the planet. These companies exist within the context of a world in crisis, intimately connected online and offline. Social Entrepreneurs will maximize the opportunity to use social technology to massively scale change.

What are the absolute basics that must be in place before any nonprofit can successfully fundraise for a cause?

It's not enough that a nonprofit's work represents something meaningful. Nonprofits need to be marketers and effective storytellers. They must clearly define a brand story, especially within their specific category. A strong and consistent message will deliver results from precious marketing dollars and provide clarity for potential donors as to why they should invest in a cause.

Second, nonprofits need to fall in love with technology, especially social media. Social media offers community-building tools for engaging and motivating their base. A nonprofit's reach, voice and fundraising can be amplified through social technology.

How can nonprofits maximize opportunities associated with social media?

Donors trade in the currency of emotion and people connect with one another around what is meaningful to them. Through the community-building toolkit offered by social media, nonprofits can tap into the emotions that motivate people to share and drive fundraising and awareness of a cause.

Do you believe there is an 80-20 rule in online fundraising?

I have a problem with the implicit idea of fundraising as transactional. Nonprofits are in the business of relationship building. If you have a strong relationship with somebody around a cause that you care about, the ability to raise funds is much easier. A nonprofit's focus should be to create a sustained community and empower this family of contributors to have a voice. These donors, in turn, become ambassadors for the nonprofit. Cultivating genuine relationships is a different emphasis with much more effective results.

What do you feel is key to creating loyal donor relationships?

In the context of so much cynicism and distrust in today's environment, consumers want to know that their hard-won dollars and heart-felt concern for a cause is actually making a difference. Look at Charity Water. Charity Water provides actual footage and uses GPS location tools to show a well being built using 100% of the donation dollars. This type of transparency is compelling. A donor's spare dollars are challenging to acquire and even worse if

100

squandered. The key to loyal relationships is transparency and accountability.

What do you know now as a leader that you wish you had known sooner?
Like many employees I travelled the world seeking work with the right company, the next big job and pay upgrade. The process of writing *We First*, however, forced me to identify what I cared about and to find my own purpose.

The entire process has given me an overwhelming and consistent feeling of gratefulness. I also feel responsibility to do something meaningful with *We First*. My "great reward" is through making a contribution to others rather than solely serving myself.

How might nonprofits move to a new level of resilience and sustainability?
The bar is higher now for nonprofits because they have effectively been given the same technology and media tools usually reserved for for-profit companies. The ability to reach and engage hundreds of thousands, millions of people, at low cost, is available. Nonprofits have less excuse now not to place greater demands on themselves. It's both a negative and a positive in the sense that nonprofits, brands and donors need to step up their game.

Is there anything else that you'd like to share?
The very concept of *We First* exists in the collective. The most effective thing we can do is celebrate each other's efforts rather than look at solutions through the lens of competition. Whether we're a brand, nonprofit, advertising agency, social entrepreneur, we are all partners in facing enormous challenges. Once we realize our business problems are a function of the barriers between us, we will more effectively be able to work together to support a cause. If we can identify our intersections, respect each other's skill sets, and complement each another, a shift from "Me First" to "We First" will occur.

If supported and directed sufficiently, this conversation around social change can become louder and louder and we might anticipate a five to ten percent shift in private sector products, over the next five to ten years.

Although every market is specific, we need to individually take responsibility for shaping the future we want. We are past the days of social media considered a fad. It's a big mistake to judge technology on the basis of how it is being used today. Social media is replacing the bliss of ignorance with the responsibility of awareness and providing tools for taking action. As such, we have incredible opportunity in front of us.

Discoveries

- Companies need the systematic integration of "giving" into their for-profit model. As an example, Contributory Consumption is a simple idea that a small portion of every product's sale is allocated to a cause in alignment with a brand's core values.
- Our business problems are more a function of the barriers between us. Once this is recognized, we will more effectively be able to work together to support a cause, whether we're a brand, nonprofit or social entrepreneur.
- Corporate Responsibility is actually innate, a core essential of being a company rather than a marketing strategy.
- In the long run, our own self-interest is best served by serving others.

Key Take Aways

- Corporations and their brands have a shared interest with consumers to improve the world: Where do your donors shop? Are there any natural affinities between a consumer brand and your cause?
- Focus on your relationship with the donor, not the transaction. Examine your website content. Are you connecting relevant stories and information to the emotions of your supporters?
- To engender loyalty, let donors know specifically how their gifts have made a difference.

Ryan Scott: Employee Engagement

"Capitalism, if applied creatively, holds the potential to transform the complex socio-economic and environmental challenges facing the world today."

-Ryan Scott, Founder & CEO of Causecast

Themes
Technology, Workplace Volunteering and Giving, Employee Engagement, Capacity Building, Corporate Philanthropy, Collaboration, Corporate Responsibility, Scale, Financial Sustainability

Profile
Type: Social Entrepreneurship
Established: 2008
Location: Los Angeles, CA
Number of employees: 30

Corporate Clients and Partners: Chegg, Virgin Mobile, AOL, *Huffington Post* (Impact and Education sections), Ben Stiller's "Stillerstrong," John Legend's "Show Me Campaign," White House initiatives "Change the Equation" and "Startup America Partnership," *CR Magazine* and AARP's "Create the Good"

Services: Causecast is the leading provider of cause integration[76] technology solutions, helping organizations become more effective corporate citizens through better employee engagement. The company's Employee Impact Platform is a one-stop shop for employee volunteering, giving, matching and rewarding, opening up new possibilities for profound corporate support of nonprofits.

The Employee Impact Platform revolutionizes employee engagement, enabling businesses to pursue ambitious corporate social responsibility (CSR) goals with automated ease while fostering a corporate culture where every employee is an inspired brand ambassador.

Mission: Causecast's mission is to enable a cutting-edge social ecosystem that elevates CSR to a new level, where sustainable and measurable accomplishments move the needle on an organization's social mission, company culture and bottom line.

Through this process, Causecast gives nonprofits the support they need to address the world's most pressing issues.

Background

In 1995, Ryan Scott co-founded NetCreations, Inc. and pioneered the "opt-in" approach for e-mail marketing. In 2001, Scott sold NetCreations for $111 million.

After observing the inefficiencies of traditional philanthropy, Scott launched Causecast to help modernize nonprofit fundraising. In 2008, Causecast introduced itself to the world at TechCrunch50, a San Francisco conference for start-ups and venture capital firms. Since then, the company has become a force in the social enterprise space, providing technology and services to help businesses of all sizes maximize their support of nonprofits.

Recognizing that the foundation of total charitable giving resides with individuals, Causecast developed a tool to unleash the full charitable potential of employees. The company's signature Employee Impact Platform helps leaders in human resources, public relations and marketing departments integrate high-value CSR initiatives into their businesses. This "turnkey" solution engages employees in uniquely collaborative cause-related work that can deepen the relationship with their employers while helping organizations improve employee recruitment and retention.

Causecast employs a unique two-pronged business approach. Revenues from Causecast's corporate clients fund the nonprofit services, allowing nonprofits to "ride free." Unlike competitive tools, nonprofits are not charged any processing fees for donations, and all other support services are complimentary. This model reflects Scott's belief that, "Capitalism, if applied creatively, holds the potential to transform the complex socio-economic and environmental challenges facing the world today."

As we'll see in his interview, Scott believes that technology, especially for employee engagement and measurement of results, holds the key to enabling expanded partnerships between companies and nonprofits.

Interview

What community does your business serve? Who are the benefactors?

Causecast speaks to four distinct audiences: business owners and managers, employees, consumers and nonprofits. For employees, our Employee Impact Platform offers innovative tools that help them improve their communities and the world while giving them a greater sense of purpose and meaning in their jobs. For employers, this interactive tool provides a special way to recruit and retain top talent. Consumers become engaged in an authentic way when workers engage their personal networks in their volunteer efforts. Above all, our platform is completely free to nonprofits and serves as an important resource to solicit the attention of their current and would-be supporters. We help clear new pathways for impact in the world, generating increased manpower and fundraising streams to nonprofits.

What brought you into this Causecast space?

After selling my first company, I wanted to give back, so I launched Causecast to help connect businesses with nonprofits. Through our work in developing public service campaigns for leading brands, I observed how even the most socially responsible companies typically under-utilize their ability to change the world. What I discovered is that perhaps the largest untapped CSR resource available to organizations is its own workforce, despite the fact that employees are the most powerful advocates for a company's cause mission. Enlisting employees in the larger social purpose of their organization not only strengthens the ability to effectively address causes, it also dramatically increases profitability through greater employee retention and consumer engagement. So I conceived of a new tool - the Employee Impact Platform - to seamlessly connect a company's workforce with its CSR initiatives, enabling organizations to propel authentic grassroots momentum that captivates employees and the public alike.

How might corporations support philanthropy?

Corporations should recognize that writing checks is only one part of philanthropy. There's so much more that most companies can do to change the world, and it starts with defining a corporate social mission. Beyond just supporting a charity, what is the organization's world view, how can it contribute to positive change, and how will the company embrace and integrate a social vision in all aspects of its work? How will the company create an inspiring work environment that prioritizes activism - whether through volunteering or donating, supporting the causes employees care about or encouraging them to champion the company's cause? To be truly effective, corporate philanthropy must be holistic, which means naturally integrating the efforts of its workforce with the company's social mission.

How do you differentiate your organization from other organizations in the same space?

It's our technology that differentiates us the most. We believe that the scale of the solution needs to match the size of the problem. Our patent-pending mobile technology, social media application, and ready-made campaigns, such as those for instant disaster relief, bring advanced solutions to help employee volunteers be as effective as possible. Combine that with our Impact Tracking technology and you've got a solution that is capable of addressing the size of the opportunity to make significant change.

How does your business collaborate with other nonprofits, other organizations, or businesses?

Causecast is growing a database of thousands of nonprofits, identifying volunteer opportunities unique to each of them that we then promote to company employees across the country. We take an active role in introducing corporate volunteers and donors to nonprofits that need their help, and we give nonprofits the technology and services to facilitate this support.

Our platform is designed specifically to connect employees and corporations to nonprofit opportunities to volunteer, donate, or simply learn more.

Which does Causecast serve more, the social entrepreneur or the nonprofit?

We serve as a liaison between employees and corporations and the nonprofit community.

How might corporations measure their societal contributions?
Measurement inherently adds value to CR programs. Sponsorships can increase if corporate donors and volunteers understand the real-world outcomes of their efforts. That's why Causecast created technology to track impact. Our "Impact Tracker" captures and measures the real-world outcomes of volunteer efforts so they can be strategically targeted to drive real progress.

In addition, we offer a product called a "Cause Integration Profile." While easy to understand and modify, each profile presents an overview of a company's charitable efforts through its marketing, employee engagement, giving and corporate responsibility programs. The Cause Integration Profile allows us to highlight these data points in one central location.

> You can view Cause Integration Profiles at:
> http://causecast.org/business

Who do you engage with on employee impact efforts?
Although the CSR industry is maturing, the contact person for philanthropy and corporate responsibility still varies within organizations. Ten years ago, a CSR title did not exist; today, employee engagement can reside within either marketing, corporate communications, human resources or corporate social responsibility.

Are there business disciplines that should be incorporated into fundraising? Why or why not?
Absolutely. I think we're learning that 'profit' in the nonprofit world is not a dirty word. It simply means 'surplus.' Having a surplus of resources - not spending them all - is a good practice, one that might even allow for the investment in necessary infrastructure needs.

Just as Causecast uses corporate fees to fund its free services for nonprofits, nonprofits are learning that earned income - selling products and services even to the people they are serving - can create a more sustainable model for change.

How do you think that nonprofits can move to a new level of self-resilience?

Nonprofits need to offer products or services that make them look more like for-profit companies or social entrepreneur-like businesses. I anticipate a collision of the three groups – companies, social entrepreneur-like businesses and nonprofits – all having a similar goal that is not defined by money. Rather, their aim will be to facilitate positive change in the lives of others through supporting causes. Any model can achieve this goal. The three models have much to learn from one another.

How do you think technology and social media has changed fundraising?

As we saw with the first Obama Presidential campaign, technology and social media have created an increase in the smaller, anonymous donor, which fosters a level of stability for nonprofits. Instead of only allocating resources towards grooming the biggest donors, nonprofits can use technology to generate a steady stream of new donors, ones that can be relied on in the future. Our participants are encouraged to leverage built-in social media tools to engage wide circles in a cause.

How does Causecast maximize opportunities associated with technology and social media?

At Causecast, social media is considered an important tool for impact. For example, Causecast provides nonprofits with action widgets to point the public towards instant donation processing and we encourage nonprofits to use this widget as a part of their social media outreach. We're standing at the epicenter of automated technology for companies and nonprofits, collecting robust data from the organizations themselves and facilitating relationships. Going forward, we're continuing to create and launch multiple platforms and track results. We maximize the actions in the database and develop opportunities in successive campaigns on other platforms as well.

Are you finding nonprofits receptive and able to keep current with new technologies?

I'm finding that the plethora of new and untested services often compete for attention. Yet only by using technology will nonprofits be able to stay on the top of their game. We are trying to build a system that is as simple and comprehensive as possible.

What have you seen to be the most successful fundraising vehicle for nonprofit organizations?
Over 90 sites offer Personal Fundraising Pages[77], a system that leverages a donor's social graph to raise money. This system works well, but these sites all charge a fee to the nonprofit. We've taken this system, moved it inside the corporation and removed the fees for nonprofits.

We also think there's great potential in the 'gamification' of charitable giving and volunteering that remains relatively untapped.

Do you feel there's an 80/20 rule in fundraising?
Although Major Donors typically do not make large gifts without a personal tie to the organization, technology and personal fundraising have led to donation sizes becoming more uniform.

What is the key to loyal donor relationships?
Provide constant feedback and communication with the donors. In a campaign to end war in Uganda, Invisible Children created constant online conversations, tweeting and streaming video over a period of seven days, with hundreds of students participating. Invisible Children had 10,000 donors giving $3 a week for a year. The enormous momentum in communication led to a successful campaign.

What do you know now as a leader that you wish you had known sooner?
It's good to be somewhat naïve about the challenges you might face. Just keep experimenting with different scenarios and solutions and eliminate the processes that don't work.

Is there anything else that you'd like to share?
Although nonprofits need to become more proficient with new technologies and innovations, there is still a stigma that equates nonprofit organizations with a lack of rigor. This is untrue. At Causecast, we help our nonprofit partners apply a for-profit business mentality to their work.

Discoveries

- Defining a company's social mission is the first step in corporate philanthropy and it's contribution to addressing the world's problems. Once a clear mission is established, it's possible to engage employees in the social purpose of the company to the benefit of the individual and corporation alike.
- Broad and deep employee engagement programs provide not only funds but capacity building opportunities for interesting collaborations and individual engagement of the employee. It's possible to quantify real outcomes of employee engagement programs.
- Success of corporate philanthropy depends upon a holistic approach, naturally integrating and synergizing the efforts of a company's workforce with a cause.
- Personal Fundraising Pages leverage an individual's "social graph" to successfully raise money.
- Nonprofits need to offer a product or service that makes them look more like a company or social entrepreneur-like business.

Key Take Aways

- Meet with a company's Human Resource department (or Marketing, Communications or CR department) to explore a broad list of employee engagement opportunities tied to donating, volunteering, capacity building and or rewarding the individual employee. What aligns with a company's philanthropic inclinations? How might employees be engaged in an empowering way?
- Carefully scale your technology to better solve the problem.
- After making a donation, ask donors to share their support on a social media platform.
- Explore "Gamification" opportunities as a potential fundraising and or community engagement idea.
- Enroll with Causecast as a corporate partner or nonprofit.

Francisco Gonima: Collaboration and Innovation

"Although people are moved by a call-to-action, well-intentioned collaborations do not succeed because the specific mechanics are not aligned with the nonprofit's core business. Sustainability occurs when collaborations are designed around an agency's core competency."

-Francisco Gonima, Arquero Consulting

Themes
Collaboration, Innovation, Self-Interest, Value Proposition, Financial Sustainability, Shared Values

Profile
Type: Consulting business incorporating "Leadership Coaching & Strategy for Turning Points, Leaps of Faith and Mighty Causes"
Location: San Antonio, Texas

Background

My interview with Francisco Gonima provided a wealth of information on collaboration and innovation. With an undergraduate degree in Latin American Studies from the University of Texas at Austin, Francisco Gonima served with AmeriCorps, a domestic "Peace Corps". Based out of a former air force base in east Denver,

Colorado, Francisco was involved in a variety of nonprofit projects, from literacy mentoring to wild land firefighting. The AmeriCorps program exposed him to multiple "discreet operating models" and the "diversity of how people arrange themselves" when collaborating or operating a nonprofit organization.

In 1998 he was assigned to work with the American Red Cross in Puerto Rico after Hurricane Georges. During the first days of disaster relief he hauled boxes. By the fourth day, Francisco was translating meetings with local mayors. By the seventh day he was coordinating the Red Cross response in two of the "municipios," or counties as we would think of them. The "bug" had caught him as Francisco discovered his aptitude for "crisis." Not only was the work invigorating, but Francisco noted the extraordinary nature of the organization.   As he says in his interview, "I was in Puerto Rico with middle class, Anglo-grandmas from Minnesota, highly educated, intellectual graduate students from New York City, a San Francisco mom who was a Chilean immigrant and an African American warehouse manager from Louisiana."   It was also easy to be enthusiastic about the Red Cross mission to relieve human suffering.   After his experience in Puerto Rico, Francisco returned to assume an official capacity by working for the American Red Cross, Mile High Chapter in Colorado.   Over the course of nine years, he took on leadership roles regionally and nationally including being a national diversity trainer, conducting inclusiveness workshops around the country.   Like so many others, Francisco fell in love with the "movement from Switzerland."

Although Francisco Gonima currently runs his own executive coaching and consulting firm, he considers himself a "Red Cross-er" for life. During our interview he shares his fluency around past and current American Red Cross innovations. We delve into the subject of collaboration: how to evaluate an opportunity, understand an organization's self-interest, and sustain a partnership. In addition, we explore the "brutal honesty of profitability" whose accompanying business values can contrast with nonprofit management.

The American Red Cross (ARC) A Perspective From Francisco Gonima

Shared Values[78]

Francisco Gonima: "As an organization, the American Red Cross has an authentic culture with heroes, mythology, rites of passage, taboos and a coded language. It's a community that unites around shared values with a capital "V," truly adopted and internalized by employees and volunteers. These become life values."

Fundamental Principles of The International Red Cross and Red Crescent Movement

Humanity The International Red Cross and Red Crescent Movement, born of a desire to bring assistance without discrimination to the wounded on the battlefield endeavors, in its international and national capacity, to prevent and alleviate human suffering wherever it may be found. Its purpose is to protect life and health and to ensure respect for the human being. It promotes mutual understanding, friendship, cooperation and lasting peace among all peoples.

Impartiality It makes **no discrimination as to nationality, race, religious beliefs, class or political opinions.** It endeavors to relieve the suffering of individuals, being guided solely by their needs, and to give priority to the most urgent cases of distress.

Neutrality In order to continue to enjoy the confidence of all, the Movement may **not take sides in hostilities or engage at any time in controversies** of a political, racial, religious or ideological nature.

Independence The Movement is independent. The **National Societies,** while auxiliaries in the humanitarian services of their governments and subject to the laws of their respective countries, **must always maintain their autonomy** so that they may be able at all times to act in accordance with the principles of the Movement.

Voluntary Service It is a voluntary relief movement **not prompted** in any manner **by desire for gain.**

Unity There can be **only one Red Cross or one Red Crescent Society in any one country.** It must be open to all. It must carry on its humanitarian work throughout its territory.

Universality The **International Red Cross and Red Crescent Movement,** in which all Societies have equal status and share equal responsibilities and duties in helping each other, **is worldwide.**

Interview

Do shared values create sustainability?
Maybe it works the other way around. Shared Values draw like-minded people to the organization that they feel reflects what's important to them. They create a vision of the world, embraced by participants as their own.

Innovation

Do you feel the American Red Cross is innovative? If so, how?
In the United States dozens of past Red Cross innovations now belong to the fabric of our society. The U.S Public Health System started as the ARC's "Town and Country Nursing Service." The Red Cross also introduced the first public ambulance services. The ARC leader, Commodore Longfellow, in the early 1900's, established the country's first standardized and publicly available swimming instruction program to stop the high number of nationwide deaths from drowning. In 1979 President Carter established the Federal Emergency Management Agency (FEMA) and it was the Red Cross that coached FEMA on transitioning from Cold War civil defense to its role today.

After 9/11, the American Red Cross spearheaded, with six other founding partners, the creation of a shared disaster case management platform, the Coordinated Assistance Network (CAN). When a victim re-tells traumatic details over and over again, they re-live the experience on a neurological level and suffer post-secondary trauma. CAN is a relational database that securely pulls authorized data from participating agency's native databases into a common portal.

114

Organizations access client information and see "apples to apples" while protecting the privacy and personal nature of the information. The human result of this breakthrough was reducing the emotional toll of disaster on recovering families by eliminating the need for them to repeatedly relive their trauma in order to access disaster recovery assistance from all available resources.

Besides introducing new technology, CAN represented a huge shift in co-creating. Instead of originating from one internal culture, change was pioneered as a collaborative. Organizations arranged themselves under the CAN umbrella for the benefit of the disaster clients.

The Founders of CAN, Coordinated Assistance Network
(http://www.can.org/our-mission)

- Alliance of Information and Referral Systems (AIRS)
- American Red Cross
- National Voluntary Organizations Active in Disaster (NVOAD)
- 9/11/ United Services Group
- Safe Horizon
- The Salvation Army
- United Way of America

Collaboration

What are the possible types of collaboration that can occur between nonprofits?
The most extreme and demanding collaboration is **joint operations**. Joint operations mean that an organization is actually integrating the delivery of services with another. For example, the Red Cross has a symbiotic, "joint operations" relationship with the Southern Baptist Convention. The Southern Baptist Convention produces and deploys mobile kitchens in support of disaster relief operations. The Red Cross purchases the unprepared food and then delivers the meals prepared by the Southern Baptist volunteers to the victims. While the Southern Baptist Convention has built competency in this

very specialized area training thousands of volunteers for cooking, it allows the Red Cross to focus on other complementary roles. In contrast to CAN, in joint operations both the Red Cross and the Southern Baptist Convention operate together with defined roles and responsibilities for each.

A second type of collaboration is **coordinated action**. In coordinated action you mutually agree to share and avoid overlap in delivery of services. Instead of one central authority, independent organizations compare services and agree on the most responsible resource deployment. Agreement can be difficult. There is anxiety about being absent from an effort: "I would love to partner with you but if clients see an American Red Cross truck and never see a Salvation Army vehicle on the scene, our brand will suffer," and vice versa. Coordinated action requires advanced marketing and communication to assure that all partners receive recognition. The deliberate design of joint branding is new territory for disaster relief efforts.

What are the best conditions for a collaborative effort?
Collaboration is not necessarily always productive. The right collaborative opportunity exists when organizations produce a "greater than the sum of its parts" return on investment of time, money and energy.

What are the questions to ask before joining a collaborative effort?
A nonprofit should first conduct an honest self-assessment. Questions include: (1) how do services complement or overlap; (2) what is the value add basis for the collaboration; (3) Can we make a long-term commitment based on the maturity of our programs and resources?

What sustains a collaborative?
Collaborations built on honestly declared self-interest endure! Although people are moved by a call-to-action, well-intentioned collaborations do not succeed because the specific mechanics are not aligned with the nonprofit's core business. Sustainability occurs when the collaborative is designed around an agency's core competency. Successful collaborations have intentional design for a long-term partnership with rigorous and honest performance metrics.

When is it time to acknowledge that a collaborative might need to end?

All collaborations should have a pre-determined, yet renewable, expiration date - a time when partners agree to evaluate performance and choose whether to continue or cease. An "expiration date" creates a sense of urgency to produce meaningful work. It's healthy to proactively demobilize a partnership that has served its purpose as opposed to allowing a poor collaboration to continually drain organizational resources like a vampire; it only dies after driving a stake through its heart!

What do you know now that you wish you had known sooner?

When I started my consulting practice five years ago, I encountered more and more social entrepreneurs. I came to appreciate the brutal honesty of profitability and offering a value proposition in the marketplace. If a product does not have value, the doors close. Nonprofits need the same internal rigor and commitment to a measurable value proposition. They need systems to evaluate and measure their real results in the world relative to the need they are trying to address and programmatic design. Like any business, long-term success depends upon metrics.

Employee "burnout" in my experience arises more from poor practices than because of the daunting nature of trying to solve social issues. The absence of effective systematic "scaffolding" to steady operating structures means that employees rely only on their willpower to hold organizational pieces together, an unsustainable practice.

Is there anything else you'd like to share?

Social enterprises resemble Rube-Goldberg machines with self-interest levers that tap consumer's natural buying patterns and drive progress against a cause. Entrepreneurs, who conventional wisdom suggests are motivated by profit, are actually more collaborative day-to-day than those in the nonprofit world or even large corporations. Social entrepreneurs have an extraordinary aptitude for sending each other business referrals and aspiring to benefits for everyone versus only focusing on profit and competition.

What are Rube-Goldberg Machines?

"A Rube Goldberg machine, device, or apparatus is a deliberately over-engineered or overdone machine that performs a very simple task in a very complex fashion, usually including a chain reaction. The expression is named after American cartoonist and inventor Rube Goldberg (1883-1970)."

Discoveries

- Collaborations based on honest self-interest endure. The most successful collaborations are designed around an agency's core competency and have rigorous and honest metrics for a long-term partnership.
- The most demanding form of collaboration is the partnering of joint operations, the integration of actual services with another organization.
- Social entrepreneurs are inherently collaborative. They aspire to help everyone versus motivated purely by profit. They concurrently strive for economic and social progress using shared values.
- Corporations have the opportunity to re-orient themselves in the market place. They can incorporate societal benefits into their value proposition, especially those principles that resonate with current customers. More and more companies recognize that business benefits when society improves as well.
- Nonprofit and government agencies must also offer a value proposition by managing resources as best as possible and developing self-sustaining practices.

Key Take Aways

- Coordinated Action is a shared delivery of service that assures no overlap. It requires deliberate joint branding. Are there ways to further your cause through Coordinated Action with organizations that complement your mission?

118

- All collaborations need a renewable expiration date. Do current partnerships have an appointed time for evaluation before renewal?
- As with Social Entrepreneurs, nonprofits need internal rigor and the commitment to offering a value proposition in the marketplace. What is your nonprofit's value proposition?

Peter Wilderotter: Building Partnerships Inside and Out

"Bill Clinton has said that 'Nearly every problem has been solved by someone, somewhere' and the solution has just not yet been taken to scale.[79] I agree. There has to be more mergers and collaboration. The rate of nonprofit creation exceeds the rate of increases in annual giving. Founders need to step aside and allow organizations to work together."

-Peter Wilderotter, President and CEO, Christopher & Dana Reeve Foundation

Themes
Collaboration, Board Management, Donor Loyalty, Strategic Planning, Organizational Structure, Behavioral Economics, Fundraising Strategies, Transitions

Profile
Type: health/medical research nonprofit
Established: 1982
Location: Short Hills, NJ
Number of Employees: 37
Budget, 2011: $18,563,000
2010 Revenue: $14,641,000
We've awarded $14,793,665 in Quality of Life grants since 1999; $90 million in research projects since 1982

Mission: The Christopher & Dana Reeve Foundation is dedicated to curing spinal cord injury by funding innovative research, and

120

improving the quality of life for people living with paralysis through grants, information and advocacy.

Background

As full disclosure, the interview with Peter Wilderotter was very near to my heart. As a family we have never stopped believing in a cure for spinal cord injury paralysis and Peter understands this passion as well. Peter is eloquent in speech and thought. As you'll see during the interview, he operates an innovative and collaborative foundation based on business principles and understanding both "the science and art" of fundraising.

Interview

How did you come into the nonprofit field and, in particular, what led you to the Reeve Foundation?
As happens to many in this field, I entered almost by accident. After a personal experience with cancer as a young child, I started in the field of nonprofit development and marketing in a series of different jobs. When recruited in 2005 by the Reeve Foundation, the organization wanted to change its "celebrity" board and extend the mission to a broader community. This challenge appealed to me.

Tell me how the Reeve Foundation differentiates itself from other nonprofits in general.
To garner support from the outside, the Reeve Foundation supports and solicits from both "sides of the ledger," in the "care" and "cure" of the spinal cord injured community. Despite an inherent tension between care and cure, we see these two groups as a distinction without a difference.

We differentiate our medical research through "open architecture," mandatory collaboration and a commitment to move research forward from "bench to bedside." The neural recovery network exemplifies our focus on bringing research results directly to the patient. Since we do not own a lab, we're able to negotiate grants with lower overhead. In addition, our scientists are required to participate in symposiums every eighteen months to share their results. Our clinical trial network insures the sharing of best practices for correctly setting up a trail. We also have a consortium of labs working together that cultivate strong post-doctorate programs, engendering future researchers to our cause.

Does the Reeve Foundation ever collaborate with other nonprofits?
Collaboration is actually in our roots. When first forming, in 1982, the founder, Hank Stifel and his "band of pioneers" reached out to other organizations and brought them together under the name, the American Paralysis Association, now the Christopher and Dana Reeve Foundation.

Our banner is "We" versus "Me" especially to maximize resources. For example, the Danny Uman Fund supported young scientists. Instead of operating separately, we created a Danny Uman Young Scientists Fund at the Reeve Foundation, thereby eliminating overhead and administrative costs and allowing more money from the fund to flow to the research. Danny also joined our board. In 2010, we also organized a symposium on aging and invited the four largest fundraisers in the field: the Miami Project, the Nielson Foundation, the Kessler Foundation and ourselves, creating much needed dialog.

What are the absolute basics that must be in place before any nonprofit can successfully fundraise for a cause?
A nonprofit needs a strong board committed to providing stewardship that reflects the adage, "Time, Talent and Treasure". Members must commit money, time and the willingness to garner knowledge about the cause. Many of the Reeve board members participate on the research committee as layman, unfamiliar with the science, but committed to probing and asking necessary questions.

Secondly, a nonprofit must have a professional staff pledged to integrity, transparency and clear business operations. In addition, nonprofits must stay committed to "who they are," their messaging, constituents and programs versus defining themselves as to "who they are not"!

What has been your most successful vehicle for raising money?
Previously, forty five percent of our income came from one, beautiful, signature gala, supported by celebrities. Over the last five years we have diversified our fundraising portfolio and built a

122

sustainable infrastructure. First, we have a broad Team Reeve concept, one including the traditional marathoner who raises money in addition to partners who host other sport-like events in their community, like the "Walk and Roll" in Harper last year. We're looking for "the fast nickels," acquiring those $10, $20, $30 dollar donations. We also shoot for "Elephants," board members donating in the six figures. Corporate foundations have helped us diversify our portfolio, too. Our Resource Center is funded through a cooperative agreement with the Center for Disease Control. We act as an out-source for the federal government, another win-win revenue strategy.

Do you feel that there's an 80-20 rule that applies to fundraising?
Everyone relies on 80-20 rules, from the clothes we wear to the sources of donations. In fundraising it can even climb to as high as 90-10, both in terms of donation size and the attention it takes to manage a significant gift.

There's an art and science to fund-raising. Science tells us that only about 5% of your donor base might make a bigger gift in the future. The science involves learned skills for thoughtfully soliciting a donor, like writing an effective letter, hosting at an event or meeting face to face. Understanding what matters to the donor, the "gut" reasons for giving, is the art. A sophisticated board and staff constantly looks to identify those that started at the $100 level but might be willing to give more.

What do you feel is the key to loyal donor relationships and what does the Reeve foundation do to maintain and cultivate these relationships?
Communication with the donors is key. An organization needs to tell donors how their gifts are being spent, the results of an organization's programs and where opportunities exist for more progress in the future. Over the last few years we resurrected a newsletter, *Progress in Research*, because we learned through focus groups that our donor base did not understand our research or its impact. Our newsletter puts a human face on the research. It tells individual stories because we believe everybody, our researchers with key breakthroughs and layman alike, have a unique story to tell.

Donors can now "touch" our cause and better understand the impact of their contributions.

How do you feel technology and social media has changed fundraising and how has the Reeve Foundation maximized the opportunities associated with technology?
Our website reflects a CNN for the spinal cord community, journalists, our Facebook and Twitter members, and our donors. Demonstrating generosity is another key website goal and includes not only recognizing donors but also providing online links to our many colleagues and partners in the field. Although we participate in all current technologies, we have yet to discern the best revenue model for online fundraising. As our web giving grows by "leaps and bounds" we are striving to determine reliable response rates, those not based only on episodic giving but on an emotional commitment to our cause.

Are there business disciplines that should be incorporated into fundraising?
Organizations must have an annual strategic plan with actions matched to objectives. Through these governance principles the board can constantly examine whether the "juice is worth the squeeze." Consistent with a business process, the Reeve board revisits our written goals at every meeting and re-evaluates before moving forward.

How do you feel corporations should support philanthropy?
Is corporate giving an oxymoron? No, companies should donate in alignment with their business interests, such as occurs with pharmaceutical companies supporting cancer or diabetes research. Corporations should strengthen their matching gift and employee volunteering programs, too. Look at Verizon Wireless in 2010 who donated over $5.5m in cash grants to nonprofits where employees volunteered and matched $13.5 million in employee donations. Corporate giving is good for the company and the community.

What do you know now as a leader that you wish you had known sooner?
From an organizational development perspective, I wish that I had better understood the relative infancy of the Reeve Foundation when I became President. At the time we had constituents aligned with

"care" and "quality of life," and others loyal to "cure" and "medical research," standing in opposite corners. We even took the word "paralysis" out of our name, reflecting an internal struggle of our organization's purpose. Our struggles were the same challenges faced by the American Caner Society forty years earlier. After five years or so, we realized that the "rising tide ought to lift all the boats," which is reflected in our current mission, "Care Today, Cure Tomorrow." Understanding the "life stage" of our organization would have facilitated a quicker, less painful, process for arriving where we are today. We not only are experiencing scientific breakthroughs but have also created a spinal cord injury movement.

"Bumps"

According to Judith Sharken Simon, author of *Five Life Stages of Nonprofit Organizations*, "bumps" as well as transitions are part of any organization's growth; "Significant events occur in each stage, and these events are necessary to move an organization forward in its development." (pg 9, Fieldstone Alliance, 2001)

How might nonprofits move to a new level of self-reliance, especially given the current economic environment?
Bill Clinton has said that "Nearly every problem has been solved by someone, somewhere" and the solution has just not yet been "taken to scale." I agree. There has to be more mergers and collaboration. The rate of nonprofit creation exceeds the rate of increases in annual giving. Founders need to step aside and allow organizations to work together.

Discoveries

- Stay true to who you are versus defining yourself by who you are not.
- Statistics suggest that only about 5% of your donor base might make a bigger gift in the future.
- Understanding what matters to the donor, "the gut reasons for giving" is the art of fundraising. Helping them "touch" the cause and better understand the impact of their donation creates loyalty. Communication with the donors is key.

- Employee matching programs and volunteering programs are all good starting points for establishing a corporate giving program.

Key Take Aways

- Demonstrate generosity and gratitude on your website by providing online links to partners in the field.
- Understand the "life stage" of the nonprofit so as to better align mission and goals.
- To allow the best ideas to surface, how might your organization build in more collaboration in its programs?
- Like a consortium of labs working towards a common cure or hosting a symposium around a common theme, what type of collaborations align well with your cause?
- Identify the mix of Time, Talent and Treasure on your board. Do you have all three?

Chapter Four – Reinvent
Foundational Principles

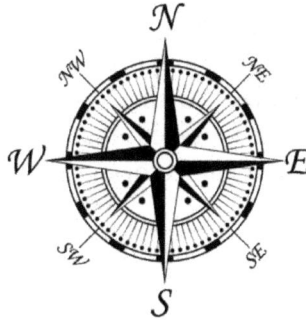

Modern infers "reinvented," examining what has worked in the past and distinguishing the best fundraising principles for today. Many of my interviewees revise and strengthen foundational practices. It's possible to distinguish yourself by simply doing what you say you're going to do, notes Eric Scroggins of Teach For America. Similarly, a "best practice" is only so if it's whole-heartedly embraced. In today's environment, we must "walk the talk!"

The Mission

Before fundraising begins, Scott Lumpkin, Vice Chancellor of the University of Denver, reminds us that a nonprofit must have clear internal and external identity, niche and purpose, defined by its mission. The mission must be easy to understand, compelling, and tangible adds Robert Wolfe, co-Founder of Crowdrise. Donors give to a cause because of its mission. Keep in mind however that in our world today, no matter how well written the mission statement, without a few key metrics that tell a compelling story, donors won't always be motivated to act.

The Board and Employees

An "army of believers," aka, a strong Board of Directors, is vital for fundraising, says John Shaw, past Chair of the Jefferies Family Scholarship, and many other interviewees agree. A board must deeply understand the organization's mission and be able to motivate others to give. Credibility is key. Peter Kiernan adds that the board must ask the tough questions and seek outside verification of the nonprofit's work. Ed Messman, Founder of Giveo, recommends that board members be progressive, understanding the impact of technology and sustainable giving ratios. Hank Stifel reminds us as well to not underestimate the referral; donors often give because they recognize a name on the Board. Rich Rainaldi, Principle of CiviCore, recognizes that the strong leaders of a nonprofit are often "Super-Connectors."

The Staff

As Peter Wilderotter, President and CEO of the Christopher and Dana Reeve Foundation recommends, it's important to recruit and retain the right people for "a professional staff pledged to integrity". To attract the most ambitious and smart demographic graduating from college, Ed Messman proposes attracting them through a hybrid-quasi-nonprofit and for-profit model, one that leverages progressive technology. If an employee is not a good fit, however, Richard Crespin, President of *Corporate Responsibility Magazine*, advises to make changes for not only the organization's good but the employee as well. Within the organizational structure, clearly identify who has the responsibility for final decisions and, Steve Daigneault suggests, empower the individual to make decisions versus tying up projects in committee.

Strategic Planning, Marketing, and Donor Loyalty

Peter Wilderotter follows a strategic plan; one that is reviewed quarterly. While setting goals is mandatory, determining how to reach targets is equally as important adds Peter Kiernan. In addition, multiple sources of revenue allow for managing transitions and creating long-term sustainability.

Developing a solid marketing strategy will uncover the natural prospects for your organization. Whether offline or online, strategies focus on connecting with donors and understanding their perspectives, regardless of "shiny" technological or traditional solicitation tools. The key to developing loyal donor relationships is to be "donor-centered," says Scott Lumpkin. Listen and understand what matters to the potential donor versus driving the conversation from the organization's perspective.

The ability to deliver a sincere and prompt thank you, personalized and acknowledged by a top person in the organization has always been important. Recognition should include results that answer the question, "Where did my money go?" with a human face as well as present a clear presentation of the gift's impact. To build a strong donor-base, Hank Stifel, reminds us that the small donor deserves sincere recognition as much as the Major Donor.

The interviews in this chapter offer a fresh look at the fundamentals (Eric Scroggins, Peter Kiernan, Scott Lumpkin, and Hank Stifel) to assure that a nonprofit not only operates effectively, but exceeds its goals.

Eric Scroggins: Defined Fundraising Plans and Relationship Growth

"Development at Teach For America is based on relationship growth. We recognize that our donors are more sophisticated than just believing in our cause. They will trust a respected source for information within their network. They usually come to Teach For America because of this trust. They stay, if we deeply engage them in our work and focus on their motivations to be involved."

-Eric Scroggins, Executive Director of Growth Strategy and Development, Teach For America

Themes
Strategic Planning, Donor Retention, Donor Engagement, Development Leadership, Metrics, Relationship Growth

Profile
Type: Education
Established: 1990
Location: New York headquarters (43 regions across the US)
Number of Employees: 1,600
Budget: $208.8M
Operating Revenue Raised in FY10 (Oct 2009-Oct 2010): $193M

Operating Revenue Raised in FY11 (Oct 2010-Oct 2011): Projected $242M

Mission: Our mission is to build the movement to eliminate educational inequity by enlisting the nation's most promising future leaders in the effort. We recruit outstanding recent college graduates and professionals who commit two years to teach in urban and rural areas and become lifelong leaders in pursuing educational excellence and equity. With extensive training and support, these corps members work relentlessly to ensure that students growing up today in low-income communities are given the educational opportunities they deserve. As alumni, they are a powerful force of leaders who act on the conviction and insight they gain from their teaching experience, working in education and all other sectors to effect the fundamental changes needed to ensure that all children have an equal chance in life.

Background

Eric Scroggins is not motivated by development as a profession. Rather, he wants to reduce inequity in education. His passion is fervently fueled by results. It's not a surprise that fundraising goals are tightly tied to programmatic impact. Although Scroggins addresses the need to raise money for new teachers and training, he views donors as more than a financial resource. Teach For America donors become integral to the movement. Fundraising goals are set high and even if sometimes, funding goals are not reached, Teach For America continues to raise the bar so long as educational disparity exists. It strives to be an organization that constantly learns and improves.

In our interview, Scroggins shares the importance of a strategic plan, metrics and entrepreneurial incentives. He re-defines the job description for a Development Director and espouses over-delivery on details and getting things right from the start. Pay attention to his responses, as they are fresh and compelling.

Interview

What does the title, Executive Director of Growth Strategy and Development, mean?
Growth and Development epitomize our model and drive fundraising. Each region asks, "What is the leadership force required to solve educational inequity in our community?" The community becomes deeply vested in funding the corps members (Growth), and, thus, motivated to raise the money (Development). Forty-three regions compete for corps members, creating a market effect and entrepreneurialism around fundraising. Benchmarks are set through four admissions deadlines and act as an added catalyst for innovation around fundraising strategies. Money must be fully secured and or confidently anticipated in the planning pipeline before corps members are allocated to a community. Benchmarks are based on "cash in," renewal rates and the weighted value of all gifts in the pipeline at the point of the funding decision.

What might other nonprofits learn from this fundraising model?
Once the toothpaste is squeezed out of the tube (and or, the admission deadlines have passed), there is no chance to put it back in! There must be meaning behind campaign deadlines. In addition, in the strategic plan, fundraising goals must directly link to program impact.

What are the absolute basics that must be in place before an organization can be successful in fundraising?
Have a vision for change and a plan that clearly communicates what the nonprofit wants to accomplish. For example, Chicago leaders might say: "We want to move from 100-400 teachers in the next three years so as to serve four times as many students, and generate four times as many alumni leaders for educational reform. Our budget will need to increase from two million to eight million dollars." The fundraising plan provides for donors' participation at multiple giving levels and directly explains the impact of their engagement and gifts. Regardless of a gift's size, donors perceive their contribution towards achieving the community's goals and connect their gift to helping the world. Our most successful Executive Directors are strong visionaries and good listeners; they are adept at making connections between potential donors' interests

and their vision and plan in concrete and inspiring ways that are appropriate given capacity to contribute (financially and otherwise).

What metrics are needed in the fundraising plan?

Each region has a funding plan. The plan identifies the goals and revenue stream from individuals, corporations, foundations and public funds. Although the broader strategy aligns with the region's vision, within those identified revenue streams are three segments: repeat donors, increased gift amounts from repeat donors and new donors.

Every solicitation needs a specific "Call to Action" that compels past donors to donate again and potential new donors to prioritize our work. Just "needing the money" is not a sufficient motivator. The "Call to Action" should provide a compelling rationale for why a donor should give a certain amount by a certain point in time that is directly related to programmatic success.

Another basic but important metric is Renewal Rates. These are indicative both of fundraising efficiency and effectiveness. Over time, Teach For America works hard to translate a donor's interest into a deeper understanding of and passion for our mission thereby solidifying the donor's connection to the organization and increasing the likelihood of renewal.

Three Segments, Three Questions

Within the funding plan, Eric Scroggins recommends answering three questions for each revenue segment:

1. How will you keep **current donors** engaged in your nonprofit? How does their renewal help the organization to accomplish its objectives?

2. Why should current **donors increase their gifts**, at this moment in time and by when?

3. What is the strategy, timing, and organizational rationale for procuring **new supporters**?

134

Los Angeles five-year plan

In order to meet the unique needs of students growing up in poverty in our target communities and to develop a robust leadership pipeline of alumni working to effect lasting change, we look to expand our presence to approximately 1,000 total corps members in Los Angeles by 2015

Los Angeles 2015 plan	2011	2012	2013*	2014	2015	Notes
						*2013 is a shortened year as we shift our FY
Corps members						
Incoming	128	225	350	375	575	
Retaining	137	118	207	322	437	90% retention
Total Corps Members	265	343	557	797	1,012	
Incoming CM Growth	-14%	76%	56%	36%	21%	
Students Impacted	19,300	25,000	40,700	58,200	73,900	
Regional Budget Estimate	$7,460,175	$9,430,000	$8,010,000	$19,400,000	$26,190,000	
Reven. Required to Raise	$112,722	$490,000	$-	$2,850,000	$1,700,000	
Budget + Incrm. Reserve	$7,572,902	$9,920,000	$8,010,000	$22,250,000	$27,890,000	$68M to be raised from FY12 - FY15
Annual Giving						
Foundations	$2,000,000	$1,700,000	$2,000,000	$2,200,000	$2,700,000	Secure 10 new/lapsed foundation supporters up to 100k
Corporations	$900,000	$1,200,000	$1,300,000	$1,400,000	$1,800,000	Maximize 25k giving level tier as an entry level point to bring in more new corporations and double corporate giving by 2015
Individual Giving (up to 199,999)	$1,100,000	$1,700,000	$2,500,000	$4,000,000	$5,000,000	Retain 80% of sponsors, annual major givers, and grow sponsor base to secure sponsorships for every corps member
State	$700,000	$550,000	$400,000	$1,200,000	$800,000	Increase CA Volunteers Grant to 800k-1M (half of FY13 grant will be applied to FY14 given shortened FY)
District Fees	$500,000	$350,000		$3,172,500	$2,472,500	Move to annual fee of $2,500 Per CM cost by 2013, district fees from 2013 will be credited towards 2014 given shortened FY
Special Events	$	$	$500,000	$750,000	$1,000,000	Corp sponsorship of events (ticketed events/sponsorship revenue)
Total Annual Giving Raised	$5,200,000	$5,500,000	$6,700,000	$12,722,500	$13,772,500	$38M from annual giving FY12-15
Growth Investor Campaign	$500,000	$5,000,000	$10,000,000	$10,000,000	$5,000,000	$30M from Growth Investors, aim is to frontload campaign with commitments FY12-14 and apply surplus to FY15
Total	$5,700,000	$10,500,000	$16,700,000	$22,722,500	$18,772,500	

Sample Fundraising Plan

135

[Regarding the Sample Fundraising Plan] "This is our most effective fundraising tool because it forces our leaders to tell a coherent, structured story about what they want to accomplish, how donors might impact specific goals, and defines the plan's key components."

What are the best ways to engage donors?
Nearly every year we increase our budget at Teach For America. This provides incentive for us to be constantly talking with our donors and the broader community, conducting conversations about our biggest organizational challenges. We see our donors as the Alumni Emeritus of our programs. They deeply understand the challenges in education and have become part of our movement. Money is critical but our donors provide so much more additional value.

We carefully bring our supporters "into the fold." Using our judgment and knowledge of a supporter's assets and background, we find meaningful and interesting ways for people to engage. For example, in our individual giving program, "Sponsor a Teacher," donors, paired with a corps member, directly experience the substance of what we do. Many long-standing relationships have ensued. Our "Sponsor a Teacher" program has been a powerful point of engagement with a strong 70% renewal rate.

Where do new donors come from?
New donors usually come from referrals, especially from those supporting a corps member. To broaden our individual donor base, we will ask our regular sponsors to help us find additional sponsors. If we have ten sponsors and each invites five more people, we then have fifty more supporters with their own networks.

Why do you believe people donate to a cause?
Development at Teach For America is based on relationship growth. We recognize that our donors are more sophisticated than just believing in our cause. They will trust a respected source for information within their network. They usually come to Teach For America because of this trust. They stay, if we deeply engage them in our work and focus on their motivations to be involved.

136

What are some of the business disciplines that should be incorporated into fundraising?

The principle fundraisers at Teach For America are not on the Development team. Rather, they are the Executive Directors (ED), who head up our 43 regions across the country. Since donors are interested in content, the ED talks fluidly about our work. Besides managing the program, the alumni and the entire office, the ED builds relationships and influences others.

The Director of Development is more like a chess player, defining strategy, assessing networks and relationships and mobilizing the various stakeholders to action. Our heads of Development are "behind the scenes," driving fundraising operations. They really understand "people's strategy," more than executing on the plan, and are exemplary in operations and management.

Secondly, "confidence is the new charisma." Our Development staff over-delivers in attention to details and execution, especially for donor cultivation and stewardship. We want our donors to feel that everything about donating to Teach For America was a memorable experience. Generally people expect good but really remember when an experience is great. To deliver the best experience for a donor, our people understand all aspects of client management, are strong writers and have strong reasoning and strategic thinking skills.

Unlike a for-profit company, nonprofits are under additional scrutiny and, instead of delivering a service, the value proposition is about solving a more complicated problem with fewer resources. Our Development leaders work as consultants in a fast-moving, complicated, quick-flowing organization, with a small margin for error.

How might nonprofits best demonstrate transparency?

First is a commitment to measuring progress. Although no measurement is perfect, we use data to drive continuous improvement over time in programs and development. Internally we track our conversion rates from prospect to donor in all our regions. We know which regions and people have the strongest conversion rates and we study our dashboards to learn more.

Measuring your results allows you to be transparent. But, it's only possible as long as you set clear goals, actually put a stake in the ground and create measurements and proxies, despite how complicated the problem is to solve. Then, regardless of the outcome, you can report back. Even if a goal isn't met, it builds credibility to proactively address what benchmarks were met and areas for improvement. Although counter-intuitive, demonstrating constant learning is helpful.

What do you know now as a leader that you wish you had known sooner?
Excellence matters. Acting on what you say you are going to do and completing the task correctly is a motivational tool because often people do not follow through.

How might nonprofits move to a new level of self-reliance?
The context for self-sustaining organizations varies greatly. We have a highly diversified funding base with high renewal rates and this has created a self-sustaining model of sorts. Although we set ambitious goals, which we to do not always reach, we still hold ourselves accountable. Fundraising the fastest way is not always most effective. Rather, instead of only asking, "How can I raise five million dollars," for example, I ask, "how might we engage the right amount of the right people?" It's much better to build capacity with twenty-five people versus being dependent upon only five. Each of the twenty-five people will bring their own network, ideas and expertise, creating much broader wealth.

Does your fundraising model reflect an 80-20 rule?
We view diversification as extremely important. Teach For America is relationship driven. Individuals contribute more than just their financial resources. We ensure our sustainability by not being overly reliant on a limited set of opportunities.

Discoveries

- Through a strong referral network, it's possible to cultivate relationship growth with the many individual donors versus a few large donors.
- New donors come from referrals. They stay because of relationship growth; understanding a donor's motivation to

be involved. While monetary contribution is critical, when donors deeply engage in the mission, they're able to add even more value to the organization.

- The Development staff works "behind the scenes," driving and managing fundraising operations while the Executive Director is the most qualified person to deliver content and ask for money.
- Meaningful campaign deadlines are mandatory to drive fundraising results.
- Transparency and metrics build credibility. Metrics proactively address goals that were met and or not met and identify areas for improvement. It's better to address what is not working than ignore it.

Key Take Aways

- Renewal solicitations need specific "Call to Actions" that connect a prior donor to their initial motivations for giving.
- Confidence is the new charisma; over deliver in attention to detail and execution, especially for donor cultivation.
- Build capacity by asking twenty-five people versus five people, for example, so as to benefit from more networks, ideas and expertise.
- Have a vision and fundraising plan that clearly communicates specific funding goals tied to program impact.
- Make sure that regardless of amount, a donor perceives the impact of a gift towards achieving a goal.

Peter Kiernan: Strategic Leadership and Business Principles

"Nonprofit management, requires a balance, in equal measure, between passion and business enterprise."

-Peter Kiernan, Past Chairman, Christopher and Dana Reeve
Foundation and The Robin Hood Foundation

Themes
Sustainable Practices, Board Management, Donor Loyalty, Marketing, Collaboration, Major Donors' Cultivation, Transition

Profile
Current: CEO of Kiernan Ventures; Chairman, TechHealth; Director, Sonostar Fund, Best Selling Author

Past Corporate: President of Cyrus Capital, a multi-billion dollar hedge fund; Chairman, Heliflite Shares;

Partner of Investment Banking, Goldman Sachs

Nonprofit: Current Chair, Finance Committee, Robin Hood Foundation; Chair, Darden School of Business, UVA; Board member of UVA College and Graduate schools; Board member, Alfred Smith Foundation

Past: Chair, Robin Hood Foundation (five years); Chair, Christopher and Dana Reeve Foundation; Co-chair, World Team Sports; Executive Committee Member, NY Center for Charter

School Excellence; Board Member, Williams College; Chair, St. Vincent's Hospital, Westchester

Background

Peter Kiernan's contributions to the nonprofit world reflect a passion play of many different roles. Throughout his life Peter watched his mother quietly suffer from MS in a discriminating world, where an invalid truly inferred "not valid" within society. In response, Peter cultivated his own civil-rights attitude in the area of disability. After Wall Street's 1987 crash, fearing long lines at the city's soup kitchens, Peter and his fellow associates felt adamant that those with resources should assist others. Thus, the Robin Hood Foundation was born. In the post 9/11 world, his generosity and passion led him to lead the Christopher and Dana Reeve Foundation, after the tragic loss of its most inspiring public leaders and namesakes.

Peter is an erudite leader with contagious energy. As we'll see consistently throughout his responses, his focus on solid business practices combined with strategic leadership is salient. The importance of board management, especially during organizational growth and or upheaval, is also a trademark of his philanthropic work.

Interview

What are the absolute basics that must be in place before any nonprofit can successfully fundraise for a cause?
Surprisingly, there is a wide range of effectiveness among organizations and many only meet a few basic requirements. Drawing from the Robin Hood Foundation, I recommend the following questions for evaluating a nonprofit's practices and identifying areas for improvement:

- Does the organization have a strong engaged leadership team?
- Does the organization have clear strategic goals?
- Do the leaders understand the mission and goals of the organization?
- What is unique about the organization?
- What are the imperatives to accomplish for the year?

- Are outcomes measureable? What analytics measure the results?
- Does the organization deliver on its programs?
- Are the organization's financials strong?
- Has the organization conducted an outside review and assessment?
- Is there any independent research to validate the organization's mission, target and programmatic success?
- Are programs cost effective?
- How do you manage your "adjacencies?"

Why is it important to examine adjacent organizations?

Kiernan suggests that a shrewder way to manage an issue and maximize resources is to identify logical collaborative partners, particularly in the Social Services sector. By working with other partners, nonprofits can extend the success of their own programs as well as eliminate a redundancy of services. Begin with identifying, "who else touches a client?"

Should nonprofits collaborate?

Yes, nonprofits should collaborate with like-minded institutions. It's a key measurement to examine because organizations will run out of money long before the issues are solved.

Look at the disability movement. Fifty-seven million people live in wheelchairs across America. Yet, efforts between organizations remain fragmented. Although Christopher Reeve and Michael J. Fox began the coalescence of a disability movement, it lacked an essential unifying voice. But, imagine the collaborative potential of fifty-seven million! Potent! Although collaboration is very difficult, it is essential for the efficient use of available resources.

What have you found to be the most successful fundraising vehicle (such as an Annual, Endowment[80], Capital Campaign[81], event, Planned Giving tools[82]?)

Successful fundraising vehicles vary depending upon whom the organization wants to reach and your organization's worldview. Organizations must segment their donor base and, then, craft a specific marketing strategy for that channel. For each channel,

142

fundraisers must decide the most cost effective way to reach it. The Robin Hood Relief Fund was able to attract corporate donations because it was the right fit. The Reeve Foundation's Paralysis Resource Center provides crucial information, meeting an outsourcing need of the federal government.

Donors interact first with a charity's brand. Realize that people will intersect with it in a variety of ways. The Reeve Foundation recognized that its younger donors were immune to traditional solicitations, like direct mail. With the creation of Team Reeve, the Foundation established a new leadership group and highly efficient way to reach these younger donors. Participating in an athletic event fit this group's needs and engaged them on a meaningful level.

Are there business disciplines that should be incorporated into fundraising? Why or why not?
Organizations need to create five or six revenue sources that coincide with the logical use of resources, budgets and forecasting models and include a web presence, outsourcing opportunities, events and specific funding groups (like the "Champions League" at the Reeve Foundation). The Reeve Foundation conducted a very successful direct mail campaign for many years. Donors responded overwhelmingly to appeals from Dana and Chris Reeve. After they died, the Foundation lost its most significant leaders, and the fundraising and advocacy apparatus needed an extreme makeover. It's funding was dependent on direct mail and an event. Without celebrity status, the Peter Kiernan's of the world could not bring in enough money. Also, with a shift to web-based strategies, our direct mail campaign went from one of the most important approaches to a meager source of revenue. Lesson learned? Diversify revenue streams.

It's a healthy discipline to subject your nonprofit to outside appraisal that scrutinizes the strategic plan, bottom line, goals and objectives etc. Exposing weakness is a good thing! The Robin Hood Foundation organized a concert to benefit the 9/11 victims. Afterwards, we reached out to the Attorney General, Elliot Spitzer, asking for a review of our work. We were the only organization, out of hundreds, to welcome oversight. Regulators do not have to be scoundrels! The Attorney General, Spitzer, agreed with our transparent practices and, as a result, repeatedly endorsed donations to our organization.

"Don't Judge a Charity by its Founder's Fame"

Last May, 2011, as Lance Armstrong, the founder of the Livestrong Foundation came under investigation, blogger Rich Polt, advised donors to understand a basic premise about Celebrity organizations: "A charity's founder, no matter how famous, isn't the measure of whether a charity is worthy of a charitable contribution." Like always, according to Polt, individuals and corporations should evaluate a nonprofit on its programmatic performance, financial stewardship and adherence to its mission. The Livestrong Foundation needs to "separate its brand from the celebrity" by communicating about its achievements to a broad base of supporters. (May 27, 2011, *The Chronicles of Philanthropy*)

Does the 80/20 Rule apply to fundraising?

As a snapshot, the 80/20 Rule might apply. But nonprofits do not live in a static photograph. They exist in a video game. Loyalty is dynamic with most reliable donors experiencing bursts of consistent giving. It's important to constantly monitor who is entering the giving space concurrently with the changing nature of the most reliable donor group.

Don't become over-reliant on a past donor group as it will change with the natural life cycle of giving. At the Darden School of Business, twenty-seven families have donated seventy-five percent of the funds. The children of these past donors are less engaged. Although no one relishes mining for new gold, an organization is perpetually charged with finding the next twenty solid rocks. As relates to the 80/20 Rule, transitions can be extremely profound.

Can you tell me more about the impact of transitions on an organization?

Transitions require rethinking of a charity's focus, how money will be raised and new messaging for the future. The board of any organization needs to build awareness around possible transitions, including a change in reliance on 80/20 or 95/5 donation scenario.

144

There are all types of transitions. My involvement in the Robin Hood Foundation was contingent upon changing what had been more of a private charity and creating a public charity; one not dependent upon a few large donors underwriting the organization but, rather a broader donor base. In the 1980's St. Vincent's Hospital in Westchester built a hospice wing for HIV/Aids patients. Thankfully, over the next decade, medical companies developed drugs that extended the life of these patients. Our board had to reassess the use of this wing. Scientific research-based foundations have to consider the transition when drugs go from "bench to bedside." Although difficult, charities should forecast and manage transitions.

Building a Military Industrial Complex[83]

Kiernan likens the broadening of a nonprofit's charitable base to the building of the Military Industrial Complex; create a stable, diverse network of supporters, resources, and organizations with a true vested, emotional and material interest in the cause. How might a coalition of donors be engaged at multiple levels, for a long time?

The notion of the traditional one-time intensive "Capital Campaign" runs counter to cultivating mutually beneficial long-term relationships. An Annual Fund[84], focused mainly on writing a check for a more undefined fund does little to truly engage a donor on a meaningful level. Foundations too, will sometimes relish spreading funds over multiple beneficiaries. This, like the traditional Annual Fund, is too retail and not only dilutes the impact but lessons the relationship structure.

What is the key to loyal donor relationships?
The key to loyal relationships relies on how effectively the nonprofit meets its mission and, in turn, touches the donor. Is the donor engaged with the organization on a real level? How meaningful is the experience?

The glue in donor relationships is transparency. The younger generation will demand it. Even well established organizations, such as United Way, whose donors in the past invested almost blindly in employee campaigns, have adapted. United Way now clearly reports how money is spent which, in turn, motivates employees to donate.

Donor relationship management also means clearly understanding and delivering on the donor's intent. Too often nonprofits will be remiss in confirming that the allocation of funds was in line with the Major Donor's wishes. Especially in an endowed situation, it's important to maintain consistent contact with the person who created the endowment. Don't let the sway of money in-hand create an independence that presumes knowledge of a donor's wishes.

About the "Glue"

Multiple research reports and consensus among interviewees in this book reiterate Peter Kiernan's premise that transparency and accompanying metrics create loyalty and improve the overall performance of a nonprofit. Consider the proposition put forward in a 2008 report by the William and Flora Hewlett Foundation and McKinsey & Company;

"Our hypothesis is that access to high-quality information will lead donors to allocate funds more strategically to organizations doing the best work. We also believe that having better performance information will help nonprofit organizations operate more effectively and better fulfill their missions. Lastly, we believe that shared information will help all nonprofit sector stakeholders to engage in constructive conversations about organizational performance and social impact."

(*The Nonprofit Marketplace; Bridging the Information Gap in Philanthropy*, 2008)

What do you know now, as a leader, that you wish you had known sooner?

Where there is smoke, there is magnum! If the Board is faced with a problem, it's usually bigger than it initially appears. Board members must ask the tough questions and have access to enough information for addressing difficult scenarios. They must apply strong business practices. All sides of the organization must demand accountability from each other. The Board must also seek outside verification of its work.

Do you have a mantra or guiding principle for leadership in nonprofits?

There needs to be a balance, in equal measure, between passion and business enterprise. In other words, on any Board, people need to know what they're talking about combined with open dialog. Any time one group has too much power unintended consequences will arise. A balance of perspectives allows effective debate and the coalescence around the right idea.

How might corporations address philanthropy?

Corporations give over 15 billion a year. Despite this large sum, corporate philanthropy is relegated to a lower level position within the corporation. And, board members only hear about the philanthropic efforts when something has gone wrong! I'd recommend that a board member oversee the company's philanthropic efforts so as to align with corporate values and return on investments.

How might nonprofits move to a new level of self-resilience?

Businesses rarely on average last more than twenty-five years whereas charities, like Cambridge University, which is over eight hundred years old, never go out of business! Board committee work provides a counter-balance to the employees of the nonprofit.

Strengthen the nomination and engagement arm of the Board and have excess capacity. A Board needs funders, leaders AND "worker bees." No member should be entitled to a role because of passion alone. Term limits and a regular turnover in board leadership are essential. Bring in new talent and provide a thorough Board package for the member to not only easily play a role but also deeply understand the nonprofit's mission. Diversity does not mean recruiting from column "a" or "b." At the Robin Hood Foundation, we have a diversity of view and experience that inhibits the possibility of an "ivory tower" approach.

Anything else you would like to share?

The nonprofit sector meets needs unmet by the government. Consider Friends of Island. It allocated $1,500 per client on Riker's Island, to a specific "re-entering" society program, and drastically changed recidivism rates from 45% to 15 %. What a brilliant return on investment compared to years of ineffectual government-run programs!

I'd support a Securities and Exchange Commission-like watchdog, in a mainly unregulated industry, to monitor the estimated 1.6 million nonprofit organizations and, with governmental funding, the almost half of trillion dollars donated each year to charities.

Discoveries

- While corporations build social goals into their operations, nonprofits might strive to create sustainable revenue sources, looking more like a social entrepreneurship.
- A shrewd way to manage an issue and maximize resources is to identify logical collaborative partners, particularly in the social services sector.
- The notion of the traditional one-time intensive "Capital Campaign" runs counter to cultivating mutually beneficial long-term relationships. For example, an Annual Fund often asks for checkbook philanthropy in return for undefined needs and little engagement.
- The key to loyal relationships relies on how effectively the nonprofit meets its mission and, in turn, touches the donor.
- Where there is smoke, there is fire! If the Board is faced with a problem, it's usually bigger than it initially appears.

Key Take Aways

- Routinely evaluate a nonprofit's practices and identify areas for improvement; Conduct an outside appraisal as well... Exposing weakness is a good thing.
- Identify "who else touches your client" for collaborative opportunities.
- Monitor who is entering the giving space concurrently with the changing nature of the most reliable donor group.
- Don't become over-reliant on prior donors as it will change with the natural life cycle of giving.
- A board member should oversee a company's philanthropic efforts versus responsibility being relegated to a lower level position.

- In the case of Major Donors, donor relationship management means understanding and delivering on the donor's intent. Don't let the sway of money in-hand create an independence that presumes knowledge of a donor's wishes.

Scott Lumpkin: Donor–Centered Practices

"The problem with an 'industrial model' of fundraising, reduced to inputs and outputs, like a factory, is that this model completely ignores the most important piece - the donor!"

-Scott R. Lumpkin, Vice Chancellor, University Advancement, University of Denver

Themes
Donor Loyalty and Retention, Fundraising Strategies, Prospect and Portfolio Management, Nonprofit Management, Marketing, Major Gifts

Profile
Established: 1864
Location: Denver, Colorado
Number of Employees: 50 ~ in University Advancement
Budget: $6 million
Type of Nonprofit: Higher Education
Money Raised in 2011 (ended June 30): $48 million
Total amount raised to date: ASCEND: The campaign for the University of Denver- $285 million
Nonprofit Experience: Past board member, National Committee on Planned Giving (NCPG, now the Partnership for Philanthropic Planning); Founding member and past president, Colorado Planned Giving Roundtable; Task Force member, NCPG, Valuation

150

Standards for Planned Gifts and Guidelines for Counting and Reporting Planned Gifts.

Mission: The University of Denver will be a great university dedicated to the public good.

Background

Imagine enjoying your work and its environment so much that you stay with the same employer for over twenty-eight years! Scott Lumpkin has spent his entire fundraising career at the University of Denver, a place that deeply connects with his values. During his career, he has interacted with almost every piece of the Advancement operation. In February 2011, he was appointed Vice Chancellor and now directs all of the University's Advancement efforts as a senior level leader.

Since he first attended the University of Denver on a scholarship, Lumpkin deeply understands the impact of donor generosity. Over the last two decades, DU has experienced phenomenal transformation, largely because of philanthropy. As a result, Lumpkin has had the opportunity to make a transformational impact. He has also directed national research projects focused on planned giving, including a landmark nationwide demographic survey of donors: *Planned Giving in the United States*. He speaks and writes regularly about gift planning and charitable tax and estate planning techniques.

Lumpkin's depth of fundraising knowledge is extensive and clear. Every answer offers a "best practice" for the reader. He presents the process for cultivating individual donors during a lifetime of giving opportunities.

Throughout the interview Lumpkin consistently offers strategies for being "Donor-Centered," the key to creating relationships, and the core of success in fundraising.

Interview

How is Advancement organized at DU and is it typical of most universities of this size?
Most universities with multiple academic divisions have a combined centralized and decentralized structure. At DU, University

Advancement represents all of the core advancement functions, including annual giving, major gifts, gift planning, corporate and foundation fundraising, donor relations, stewardship, gifts and records, prospect research and prospect management. As part of our extended team, fundraisers are embedded in various academic units, such as law, business, and international studies, with the fundraisers in those units reporting to their respective deans. Centrally we raise just as much money for those academic units as their own teams might achieve; that's because we're collaborative and focus on reaching the donor's objectives for what they want to support at the university. Sometimes we take the lead role and at other times we provide support. Collectively, we have two-dozen Major Gift fundraisers, including myself, who carry portfolios of individual prospective donors. That may sound like a lot, but we are actually lean in comparison to our peers.

Advancement versus Development

In higher education, Advancement is synonymous with Development. Sometimes the fundraising department of a university might be called "Institutional Advancement." Although fundraising represents the core focus, frequently "Advancement" will also encompass Alumni Relations, External Relations, and even, marketing and communications, other areas that "advance" the university itself. In contrast, at most nonprofits, outside of higher education, fundraising is found within "Development."

Which nonprofits do the best job at differentiating themselves and how is it accomplished?

The best nonprofits have a clear internal and external sense of identity, niche and purpose with everybody moving in the same direction with that mission. During the University of Denver's one hundred and fifty year old history, we have had, at times, an inconsistent identity. Our last chancellor, Dan Ritchie, pushed us to embrace the vision of a great private university dedicated to the public good. It's short, easy to understand and directs our actions. For example, even though we could be much larger, DU caps the freshman class size to keep classes small and maximize student faculty interaction. We also actively encourage and support community service efforts around the world. That's part of delivering on our mission.

How do organizations differentiate themselves from others delivering a similar product and or mission?
Look at ways to innovate within your specific niche. Corporations apply this principle repeatedly. As an example, the University of Denver interviews every single freshman applicant. That's very unusual, but it's in line with our values. We want that student to know that DU cares about them as a person.

What absolute basics must be in place before any organization can successfully fundraise?
In addition to a clear mission, it's critical to have prospects. If nobody is willing to buy your product, the organization will struggle. A nonprofit, especially just starting, must ask, "Who are our natural targets and have we sufficiently developed the relationships to start capturing and developing their philanthropic potential?"

Having a dedicated core of leaders, volunteers and, even donors, is crucial, too. They can generate momentum for an organization and motivate others to join. A successful track record of delivering on the mission must be in place as well.

What is the key to developing loyal donors?
The biggest, single answer is being "donor-centered." It's about being respectful and patient enough to sit down and listen to each donor's story without any preconceived notions or agenda. Too many fundraisers make the mistake of driving the conversation from the organization's perspective. Understanding a donor's interests, motivations, and values creates loyalty. Once you understand what matters to the donor, then it's time to explore ways that your organization's needs might match their interests.

What have you seen to be the most successful fundraising vehicles, the best tools, for raising money?
There is not just one "best way" to raise money. Fundraising strategies should be matched to what the organization is trying to accomplish and the donor's individual priorities. One fundraising

strategy isn't more important than any other; they're all critical and tied to each other.

If the purpose is to generate connections, involve people, and engage the maximum number of donors, then annual giving strategies such as direct marketing, phoning, and social media might be the best choice. If the goal is to make a transformational impact on an organization, planned/major gifts strategies should be utilized.

The National Committee on Planned Giving conducted a landmark demographic survey of donors and observed a direct correlation between people that give year after year and those that create a bequest[85] in their will. It makes sense that loyal, annual donors would consider adding an organization to their estate plans. Their devotion is deep enough that they're practically elevating the charity to the level of a family member.

Fundraisers need to integrate Gift Planning and Major Gifts and not limit themselves only to soliciting outright gifts of cash. Gift Planning and Major Gifts are not two separate areas but rather represent different dimensions of a gift. "Major Gifts" suggest "size" and "Gift Planning" describes "how" a gift will be made.

A "Donor-Centered" Conversation

When approaching a potential supporter, start with questions such as:

"Tell me your story; why did you come here today; what is important for me to know?"

Find out what matters to the donor. What motivates them? What are their interests? Values? What kind of direction and strategy do donors want to employ for their gift? What is their timing? Genuinely listen and be truly interested in what matters to them.

Do you have a sense that there is an 80-20 rule in fundraising?
For universities, especially those focused on Major Gifts, it's even greater; 90-10 or even more.

How might organizations maximize the opportunities associated with technology and social media?

Every best practice charity utilizes information management systems for donor information and gifts and records. E-mail is used extensively to drive donors back to a website and make it easy for them to give or engage at a deeper level. The use of social media at the university level is not extensive but might be used for targeting young alumni, for instance.

Another use of technology is in basic target marketing, segmenting your database into constituent groups and then customizing the messages and marketing strategies accordingly. Several years ago we re-designed our Gift Planning marketing by focusing on loyal donors, those that had made gifts for ten to fifteen years or more. Instead of calling on someone over a certain age, our Gift Planners focused on the most loyal donors, even if they were only 45.

Did you know?

"The average age when somebody first puts a charity in their will is 49."

-Scott Lumpkin, Vice Chancellor, University of Denver, University Advancement

---

Are there business disciplines that should be incorporated into fundraising? Why or why not?

Absolutely! Every sales person, aka Major Gift Officer, must have a clear portfolio of prospects that are prioritized and ranked in a plan. Then, build in accountability and examine if they are taking the right actions to lead to a sale. Sales management questions to consider include:

- How man telephone calls are made?
- How many personal visits occurred with a potential donor?
- Are proposals being submitted?
- What are their results?
- What is their close rate?
- Have prospects been identified and qualified?

- What dollar amount can be applied to their prospect list?

Developing successful Major Gift fundraisers starts with focusing on what matters and can be controlled. Fundraisers can't control whether or not someone decides to donate and the size of the gift. But they can manage their time in developing relationships with the best possible prospects.

It's easy to slip into the mindset that fundraising is all about numbers, like an industrial process driven entirely by metrics. Major gift fundraising, however, can't be reduced to a system of inputs and outputs. Metrics alone do not define donor relationships.

At the end of the day, it is possible to control how actions are prioritized. Actions, in all cases, must be donor-centered. It's a good idea to incorporate more subjective measures, such as progress within a donor relationship during a year...that's both observable and meaningful.

How might corporations support philanthropy?
While corporations have their niche in philanthropy, our focus is on individuals; that's where the wealth lies. Individual donors are responsible for more than seventy-five percent of all charitable gifts, and, when you add in bequests, the number approaches more than eighty percent. Foundations are another important source of funds and, in today's growing world of family foundations, may simply represent a creative vehicle for individual and family philanthropy.

Giving USA: 2010 Contributions[86]	
Individuals	$ 211.77 billion (73%)
Foundations	$ 41.00 billion (14%)
Bequests	$ 22.83 billion (8%)
Corporations	$ 15.29 billion (5%)
Total Giving	**$ 290.89 billion**

What role should government play in supporting nonprofits?
Government should recognize the important role of nonprofits in our society. Our tax code uniquely encourages philanthropy but changes to the tax code can also discourage giving and have a damaging effect on nonprofits. Charities demonstrate their accountability by reporting their activities on IRS Form 990. Although it can take significant organizational resources to complete, this form is an important tool for assessing a nonprofit's operations

Have you seen any successful collaboration between nonprofits sharing a similar mission?
In terms of general cause marketing, I recently moderated a panel of five institutions belonging to Denver's Scientific and Cultural Facilities District. The CEO(s) addressed major gift donors about the collective importance of science and cultural entities within the city. By speaking together with one voice, they jointly encouraged greater philanthropy in this sector.

How do feel nonprofits can move to a new level of self-resilience?
The starting place for fundraising is being "donor-centered." From there, you move donors to a different level of investment, from gifts of income to gifts of assets, increasing the organization's financial ability to withstand drops in funding and deepening the level of commitment from the closest stakeholders.

Is there a mantra that you as a leader aspire to?
My dream is to create a culture of philanthropy that is evident at our core, part of who we are as students, faculty, staff, parents and alumni. It requires being donor-centered consistently in our approach. We have a poor annual giving rate because we have "stopped and started" in our investment to encourage these donations. My vision is greater annual participation at all levels and a stronger donor base.

Is there anything else that you would like to share?
Baby Boomers represent a significant segment of our society and they think differently about philanthropy. Instead of making general, unrestricted gifts, they focus more on restricted gifts and their impact. Organizations that emphasize the importance of donor impact will be better positioned to weather changes in the future. Although taxes might affect the size of a gift, giving is not just for

157

tax benefits. Giving is about an individual's choice to make our world a better place. That's what matters.

Discoveries

- Being "Donor-Centered" creates loyal donor relationships and is at the core of success in fundraising. In other words, fundraising strategies should be matched to what the nonprofit wants to accomplish and a donor's priorities.
- Fundraisers need to integrate Gift Planning and Major Gifts, which represent different dimensions of a gift and not limit themselves to only soliciting outright gifts of cash.
- In philanthropy, the money and wealth resides with the individual donor.
- Baby Boomers focus more on restricted gifts with clearly defined objectives than on unrestricted giving opportunities.

Key Take Aways

- To uncover prospects, identify first the natural targets for the nonprofit and how to sufficiently develop those relationships.
- Find out what matters to the donor. What motivates them? What are their interests? Values? Timing? And what kind of strategy do they want to employ for their gift?
- Every Major Gift Officer must have a clear portfolio of prospects that are prioritized in a plan with clear accountability and measureable action steps.
- Organizations that emphasize donor impact will be better positioned to weather future uncertainty in the nonprofit sector.
- Remember that giving is about an individual's choice to make the world a better place.

Henry G. Stifel: Structure and Recognition

"Don't forget to include a return envelope with your marketing activities!"

- Henry G. "Hank" Stifel, Founder, Stifel Paralysis Research Foundation

Themes
Board Management, Nonprofit Start-Up, Organizational Structure, Donor Loyalty and Recognition, Sales Practices, Major Donors

Profile
Type: Nonprofit

Business Experience: Vari-typer Corporation, Xerox of Canada, Armotek Industries, Chairman and CEO

Nonprofit Experience: Founder of the Stifel Paralysis Research Foundation; former Chair of the American Paralysis Association; Director Emeritus of the Christopher and Dana Reeve Foundation; past Board Member of Choate Rosemary Hall, The Pingry School, Christ Church, Summit, NJ; current Trustee of the Vero Beach Museum of Art, The National Museum of Wildlife Art, and the Indian River Land Trust.

Background

It's my hope that, in my family, the apple doesn't fall far from the tree. My father, Henry G. Stifel, aka "Hank," exemplifies giving back to his community, in the broadest sense of generosity. Like many others, Hank entered the nonprofit field after a tragedy.

In 1982, at the age of seventeen, my brother suffered a spinal cord injury in a car accident, leaving him paralyzed from the neck-down. The doctor's prognosis was bleak. When faced with the prospect that his only son would never walk again, my father, supported by family and friends, fought back. He established a family foundation to find a cure. Although Hank had volunteered previously in his community, the accident took his philanthropic commitment to a new level, searching for cures not only for my brother but accessible to all that suffered a spinal cord injury. He and his many supporters paved the way for the field of spinal cord injury research that exists today.

In this interview, Hank speaks of authentic, tried and true principles in fundraising, based on a world less tied to technology and more connected on a personal level. He discusses basic business and sales practices, combined with recommendations on how to "touch" a donor and empower a board.

Interview

How did you start the Stifel Paralysis Research Foundation?
After my son, Henry, suffered a spinal cord injury and we were told that he would be in a wheelchair for the rest of his life, my family, friends and I rallied around. We said, "To hell with that! We are going to find a cure for paralysis."

Despite the fact that little research existed at the time, we had the sympathy and support of dear close friends and, as word spread of our goal to fund research, others affected by spinal cord injury, whom we had never met before, became involved. We took advantage of that support, formed a board and set up an office in our son's bedroom! After a year, we established an offsite office and hired an Executive Director.

What do you believe are the absolute basics that must be in place before any organization can successfully fundraise for a cause?
First, an organization needs a clear mission statement that explains why the organization exists. Second, with a strong Board of Directors, a nonprofit needs a competent Executive Director, followed by a Development Director and a Marketing Director. Third, an organization must be able to report and verify results through a financial audit, preferably conducted by an outside firm.

160

What are the best, most successful vehicles for raising funds?
Cultivating potential Major Donors, through your personal and professional contacts and those of board members, is the most effective way to raise money. Although it's much more time consuming, a second, almost equally important way to raise money is through a fundraising event. An event builds community and your donor base, and it also generates positive publicity for the organization. But keep in mind that one donor can often generate as much or more money than one event.

Do you have a sense that an 80/20 rule applies to fundraising?
It's like income taxes! Ten large donors might represent the majority of your donations. But, keep in mind, even the smallest donation deserves as much respect and recognition as the largest gift.

What is the key to creating loyal donor relationships?
At a minimum, I recommend delivering a sincere and prompt written thank you note, signed by a top person in the organization, such as the Chairman of the Board. The thank you must be personal. When I receive an acknowledgement written as "Dear Henry" versus "Dear Hank," the thank you is impersonal and I know that the organization doesn't know me. Phoning donors with the sole intention of thanking them for their gift also creates loyalty, especially since most organizations usually only use phone communication for solicitation. This is particularly true when board members make these calls or hand write brief notes on more formal thank you cards. Since so few organizations call to say "thank you", donors might almost be in shock and will remember the extra effort the next time they receive a solicitation: "Hey, that's the organization that called me to say 'thank you'."

How have technology and social media changed fundraising?
Technology can never replace direct contact for effectively selling a cause or saying "thank you," whether on the phone, through the mail, or in person. Organizations need to remember that giving is personal and touching potential Major Donors with thoughtful, sincere communication is mandatory.

It's hard to imagine that Major Donors, ones making "Major Gifts" ranging from ten thousand to million dollar donations, sit in front of their computers perusing nonprofit websites and then respond to email solicitations or online campaigns. There is little that is personal in this type of outreach. Frankly, organizations must guard against lazy online communication, against outreach that has little meaning or punch. Again, put the Directors and large supporters to work.

When you look at the nonprofit community, which organizations do the best job differentiating themselves and why?

The organizations that stand out have an active and empowered board, always listed prominently on the organization's letterhead. The board is charged with helping the organization fundraise. Membership is based not only on knowledge around a cause but also on a member's contacts and financial ability to make a contribution. The Development Director or Executive Director should know how to utilize their board, including communicating financial expectations. After reviewing the letterhead's list of directors, donors will feel motivated and almost compelled to give if they have a friend on the board and or recognize a name. It's a form of peer pressure that works and a prime reason for listing names of board members.

Are there business disciplines that should be incorporated into fundraising? Why or why not?

A not-for-profit should be run just like a for-profit business, but with different titles. The organization needs a Sales Manager, aka, a Development Director. The Development Director raises money and constantly sells a particular product, which is the cause. The mission statement must be repeated and repeated and repeated or, in other words, well marketed, including public relations such as press releases and publications. There needs to be a strong organizational structure with a leader, the Executive Director, and paid employees, including Sales and Marketing staff, who know, among other things, how to utilize the board. In addition, nonprofits need a controller who provides audited financials, thus creating transparency for its donors.

How might corporations support philanthropy?

If nonprofits want corporate participation, they must directly solicit corporate support. If a feeling exists today that corporations don't do enough, it's because they haven't been asked. Corporations like to support charities because it's good PR for the firm.

162

How might a nonprofit approach a corporation?
First, speak only with a top guy. Utilize your contacts and those of your board members and friends to reach the CEO and set up a brief meeting. Tell he or she the organization's story and ask personally for their support. Enlist a corporation's name to your cause and ask the CEO if he/she might be listed as a member of an "Advisory Board" with no obligation but with their obvious approval of the organization's mission. This equates to listing their name on the letterhead, thereby adding credibility to the organization. Although possible at the first meeting, the next step is to broaden that individual's role in the organization, perhaps as a new member of the board. If approached personally, most people will agree to participate.

Have you seen any successful collaboration between nonprofits sharing a similar mission?
Despite a competitive environment to raise money, the best nonprofits seek out similar organizations and identify how they might work together. Often too many egos are involved and organizations are not willing to render any perceived loss of independence. Collaborative efforts must emanate from the nonprofit's Chairman, Executive Director or leaders on the board.

What do you know now, as a leader, that you wish you had known sooner?
Successful not-for-profits operate very much like for-profit businesses, only with different terminology. Treating a not-for-profit organization like a business is key while realizing that your profits translate as the societal benefits provided by the nonprofit.

Is there anything else you'd like to add?
Concerning board management, there should be term limits for members. A three- year term works well with perhaps the option for an additional three-year term. Board responsibilities should be clearly defined and communicated. The title of "Chair" carries the most prestige and should be maximized for thanking Major Gift donors and cultivating new contacts.

Discoveries

- Even if Major Donors represent the majority of an organization's charitable gifts, keep in mind that the small donor deserves respect and recognition, too. Get to know your donors!
- Technology can't replace personal contact. Whether online or in person, communication needs to touch the donor.
- Despite a large time commitment, events build community, your donor base and publicity and should be prioritized in conjunction with Major Donor cultivation.
- As a start up, a nonprofit needs a strong mission and organizational structure including: a Board of Directors, Executive Director, Development Director and Marketing Director (authors note: add an IT Director as well)

Key Take Aways

- Enlist board members in thanking Major Donors with thoughtful and personal thank you(s), such as a phone call or a personal note and or signed by the Chair of the Board. Small gestures often make for big results!
- List board members prominently as peer pressure and referrals sway donors.
- Add credibility to the organization by seeking out CEO's and enlisting their names for an "Advisory Board."
- How is the small donor acknowledged? Is recognition credible?

Chapter Five – Build Sustainability

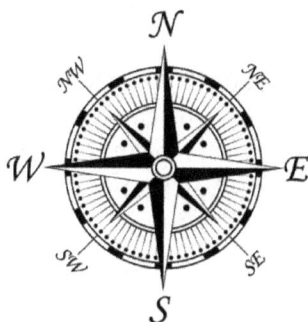

The interviews in *Fundraising Innovators* provide us with fresh strategies and tactics for achieving fundraising success. After all, money matters! As these experts have demonstrated however, today's fundraising practices can have even broader impact on the organization and community. If a nonprofit applies these new practices highlighted in the interviews to its fundraising, independence and self-reliance will ensue.

It is possible therefore that fundraising can build sustainability. In this chapter the new and reinvented practices presented in the interviews are synthesized into a ten-point manifesto on how to achieve sustainability. Recurring revenue, if smartly solicited and stewarded, means that nonprofits no longer need operate from a deficit. Successful funding finances a nonprofit's programs, enabling its mission.

As discussed in the previous four chapters, the following ten principles have emerged. Taken together they provide a pathway to sustainability. Given their potential benefits to your organization, let's review with an emphasis on implementation.

1. Operate from a "Donor-Centered Perspective"

When meeting with a potential donor, listen first. Uncover the myriad of reasons for a gift and how best to match a donor's generosity and resources (not only cash) with the nonprofit's needs.

2. Embrace Current Technology

Embrace current technology to advance constituent relationships and identify key metrics. Although tracking quantitative results on the probability of a donation is important, qualitative measurements around engagement have become equally relevant, measuring how much a donor has been engaged in meetings or online. Technology also provides more measurement capabilities so that nonprofits can analyze their programmatic, marketing and fundraising success and provide the donor with a few key metrics.

3. Engage Donors Online

Engage more donors online in new and interesting ways through the use of technology, including social media, e-mail and digital tools, thereby cultivating a broader base and reducing the reliance on a 95/5 giving ratio. In the interviews we came to appreciate that the higher the giving ratio, the more susceptible the revenue base. Designing relevant and personal fundraising and outreach campaigns to different donor segments, online and offline, will address the dichotomy of needs, especially between the million dollar donor and the smaller, younger contributor.

As Eric Scroggins of *Teach for America* reminded us, it is important to embrace "the right amount of the right people." Referrals are a reliable way to build a donor base, too. In addition, if possible, avoid "black holes" in fundraising by adding as much definition as possible to campaigns, even in an Annual Fund. The more defined the appeal, the better success of a campaign. Donors want value with their gift, something that clearly answers "what's in it for me?"

4. Integrate a Compelling Marketing Message.

Propagate a consistent and compelling marketing message by internally synchronizing different departments and externally integrating offline and online marketing. In many interviews it became clear that passion and a mission statement alone are not enough to sustain an organization. Rather, similar to a business or a social entrepreneurship, providing a consistent value proposition in the nonprofit sector matters as much as the mission.

166

5. Create a Hybrid Nonprofit-for-Profit Revenue Model

Determine multiple revenue sources, and even create a hybrid nonprofit-profit model. "Value" can also mean offering something like a product or service, as an additional source of revenue. The nonprofit, Network for Good, has multiple revenue sources, allowing it to be self-sustaining.

6. Collaborate with Other Change Partners

Work with other change partners ("competing" nonprofits, social entrepreneurs, corporations) to better utilize resources and generate innovation. Social entrepreneurs, like *Giveo* and *Crowdrise*, show us that it's possible to affect positive change and make a profit as well. The Red Cross has consistently created innovation by working with other organizations.

7. Engage Corporations

Engage the employees of a company and build long-term alignment with corporations, making profit and philanthropy synonymous. Corporations can build capacity in areas like accounting, marketing, human resources and technology. Conversely, nonprofits can help companies identify logical intersections of cause with profit.

8. Address your Organization's Weaknesses

The expanded use of the Internet has created the need for greater openness. Like a third party audit, transparency is in everyone's best interest. Increased transparency will enable nonprofit boards to make tough decisions. In addition, donors will appreciate a candid nonprofit versus learning about mismanagement after the fact.

9. Refresh Leadership

Refresh and reinvigorate the leadership, employees, supporters and volunteers of an organization as often as possible. Boards must be strengthened with term limits, regular turnover and new talent. To attract inspired employees, nonprofits should offer an entrepreneurial work environment with a progressive culture; one that strives to constantly innovate.

10. Aggressively Utilize a Strategic Plan

Aggressively utilize a Strategic Plan to achieve goals. To be effective, nonprofits need to constantly evaluate their internal processes and success at meeting goals. They need to examine their programs in order to consciously move their mission forward

Chapter Six – A Fundraising Innovators Action Plan

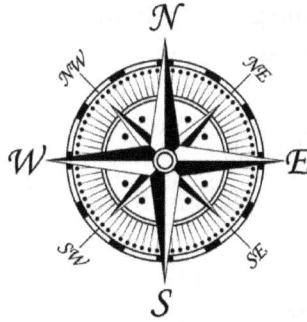

The following suggested "Action" steps are derived from the interviews and tie to the specific questions and categories of the book. My hope is that the reader will digest and translate the thought-provoking research and theory from this book into actionable and realistic steps. Since every organization has its own unique opportunities and challenges, I'd recommend starting with your business plan and customizing these recommendations to strategic goals. The plan has **seven sections**: (1) Technology, (2) Integrated Marketing, (3) Social Media, (4) Corporate Philanthropy and Collaboration, (5) Reinvented Best Practices in Fundraising, (6) Donor Loyalty, and (7) Additional Sustainable Practices.

(1) Technology

I. Does your organization have a basic technology structure in place? This includes the following:

- Constituent Management Platforms, including CRM's, to facilitate a constituent development plan, especially for uncovering new prospects and advancing current relationships with Major Donors, and to establish programmatic metrics.
- A strong Website which affords essential components (see below)
- Transaction capabilities that support one-time and recurring donations, honorary and memorial giving, and large gifts without limits. Is there an option for directing funds? How about "Ask' strings for returning donors?
- Is E-mail able to be effectively utilized, including relevant segmentation?
- Do you have Peer-To-Peer fundraising competency?

II. Analyze your website

- Does it present a strong impression of management?
- Is it easy to make a donation?
- Are financials easily accessible?
- Do you present the why care, what needs, why now?
- Will your donor want to give after experiencing your website?
- Do you have third party endorsements?
- Is your website "responsive to" your constituents?
- Are you connecting your content and or stories to the emotions of the supporter?
- How does your website demonstrate generosity to your community? Do you provide helpful links to partners?

III. Create a Technology Plan for your organization

- Does technology advance the mission of your organization?
- Examine business strategy to determine how technology will be prioritized in the organization.

- Include an analysis of IT Staffing in your plan.
- Does IT have representation on the Executive Board?

Resources for Technology

Planning

http://www.nten.org/learn/bytopic/planning

http://www.techsoup.org/learningcenter/techplan/index.cfm

A Webinar and template, "Tips and Tools for Tech Planning," from TechSoup: http://www.webjunction.org/techatlas

"Assess your Tech: Why Nonprofits Need Technology Assessments: Developing a Sustainable technology plan starts with a thorough assessment:"
http://www.techsoup.org/learningcenter/techplan/page12082.cfm

"Creating a Technology Advisory Committee at Your Nonprofit: You don't have to go alone:"
http://www.techsoup.org/learningcenter/techplan/page11356.cfm

"Writing Nonprofit IT Policies and Procedures: Use IT to improve communication, set priorities and manage expectations:"
http://www.techsoup.org/learningcenter/techplan/page11186.cfm

"The Purposeful Techie: Nonprofit IT with Intention:"
http://www.techsoup.org/learningcenter/techplan/page10549.cfm

"Use Strategic Technology Planning as a Fundraising Tool:"
http://www.techsoup.org/learningcenter/techplan/page5499.cfm

Managing Technology to Meet Your Mission: A Strategic Guide for Nonprofit Leaders. Editors: Holly Ross, Katrin Verclas and Alison Levine; Jossey-Bass, A Wiley Imprint, 2009

Constituent Management Platforms

"Multiple Constituent Groups, One Database: Case Studies" by Chris Bernard, December, 2011:
http://idealware.org/articles/multiple-constituent-groups-one-database-case-studies

Consumers Guide to Low Cost Donor Management Systems, June, 2011, by NTEN and Idealware:
http://idealware.org/reports/consumers-guide-low-cost-donor-management-systems?key=48715630

"Do You Need a New Donor Management System? A Step-By-Step Decision-Making Workbook", March 2011 by TechSoup Global and Idealware:
http://seminars.idealware.org/documents/donor_management_workbook_v3.pdf

Website Strategy

A Website Ecosystem:
http://www.bluetoad.com/publication/?i=90086

"Nonprofit Website Fundamentals; Building a Website that Supports Your Mission." By Convio, 2010:
http://conviosummit2011.com/?wpfb_dl=478

What are Web Widgets:
http://webtrends.about.com/od/widgets/a/what_is_widget.htm

"Ten Most Popular Blogs" by Elize Moreau, About.com;
http://webtrends.about.com/od/profile1/tp/Top-10-Most-Popular-Blogs.htm

(2) Integrated Marketing

- Create an Integrated Marketing Plan to assure consistent messaging across all channels, for the small donor and Major Donor.
  - Use integration to direct donors to take additional actions (like follow-up after an event, or an e-mail after a direct mail piece).
  - Does your organization's leadership support departments internally working together?
  - Include a comprehensive communications calendar
- Analyze and track data to understand how donors respond to different channels and then segment and market accordingly. These metrics should also help analyze the lifetime value of a donor, across all marketing channels.
- Analyze quantitative results from a campaign, online and offline, and build the learning into the next campaign.
- Provide meaningful stories, repeatedly, on the impact of a donation, for both online and offline outreach.

Online Marketing

- Incorporate visual indicators, like Badging systems, Thermometers or something specific to a campaign, to communicate news, engagement or progress on a goal.
- Design specific relationship building plans for segments best suited for online engagement. Regardless of campaign type, be clear about your analytics up front.
- Analyze your e-mail communications. Are your messages relevant and sent to the appropriate segment?

Other Digital Tools

- Is there a logical point of daily interaction with your donor, when it's possible to elicit an emotional connection? When text messaging or other technology might be applied?
- After donors make a gift, utilize various tools, like video and audio, to demonstrate gratitude.

Resources for Integrated Marketing

Tracking and Analyzing Data

See blog of the Integrated Marketing Advisory Board. Recent posts include a definition of "What Integrate Marketing Means to Me," http://www.imabgroup.net/

"2011 DonorCentrics Internet and Multichannel Giving Benchmarking Report" by Helen Flannery and Rob Harris, Target Analytics, a Blackbaud Company, July 2011, Charleston, SC: https://www.blackbaud.com/analytics/multichannel-giving.aspx

"Data and Storytelling: 6 Ways to Use Data to Move Your Mission" by Kurt Voekler, CTO, Forum One, May 12, 2011, NTEN blog, http://www.nten.org/articles/2011/data-and-storytelling-6-ways-to-use-data-to-move-your-mission

Visual Indicators and Badging Information

"Visual Storytelling for Nonprofits" by Christy Wiles, Marketing Manager, PhotoPhilanthropy. NTEN blog, October 4, 2011 (http://www.nten.org/articles/2011/visual-storytelling-for-nonprofits)

Content Strategy

"Your Top Ten Content Strategy Questions" by Michaela Hackner, Forum One Communications, Oct. 6th, 2011: http://www.nten.org/articles/2011/your-top-10-content-strategy-questions-finally-answered

"Storytelling Best Practices: Website" by Andy Goodman: http://www.agoodmanonline.com/newsletter/Storytelling_Best_Practices_Websites.pdf

"Top the Web Search list, Pt. 1" by Lance Trebesch, Taylor Robinson and Denise Moorehead- Foundations of SEO Strategy. Tips for building the foundations of your SEO strategy.

174

http://www.tsne.org/site/c.ghLUK3PCLoF/b.3508731/k.E42C/Articl
es__Search_Engine_Optimization_Directories_Keywords_and_Web
_Content.htm

"Understanding Web Analytics" by Laura Quinn, Founder and Director, Idealware; Third Sector New England

http://www.tsne.org/site/c.ghLUK3PCLoF/b.3362427/k.4534/Articl
es__Understanding_Web_Analytics_A_Primer_for_Your_Nonprofit
_Organization.htm

"How to Design a Nonprofit Website that Engages Donors and Volunteers," by Stephanie Hamilton, January 18th, 2012, The Daily Egg:
http://blog.crazyegg.com/2012/01/19/design-nonprofit-website/

Email

"The Role of Email in Your Communications Mix," by Heather Gardner-Madras, July, 2009;
http://www.idealware.org/articles/email_comm_mix.php

"A Few Good Broadcast Email Tools," by Laura S. Quinn, March, 2010;
http://www.idealware.org/articles/fgt_email_newsletter_tools.php

(3) Social Media

- After making sure that your organization's website is well organized and e-mail capabilities are established, design a specific Social Media Plan with measureable goals (such as building reach and increasing responsiveness of "friends") and aligned with business strategy.
  - Locate and understand where your supporters congregate. Use RSS Feeds to listen and design meaningful content.
  - Use multiple social media sites to recognize donors. Conversely, ask donors to share their donations about their gift with "friends."
  - Once you've identified your audiences, follow the 1-99 rule: truly commit to the 1% in engagement.

Resources for Social Media

The Networked Nonprofit: Connecting with Social Media to Drive Change by Beth Kanter and Allison H. Fine, June, 2010

"Going Social: Tapping into Social Media for Nonprofit Success," Convio, 2010;
http://www.councilofnonprofits.org/files/Convio_Social-Media-Guide.pdf

"Building Your Social Media Fan Base," By Laura S. Quinn, October, 2011http://www.idealware.org/articles/building-your-social-media-fan-base

(4) Corporate Philanthropy and Collaboration

Corporate Philanthropy

- Confirm that your Matching Gift program is well organized. Determine the "hook" for engaging companies is this program. Create an "Ask" that demonstrates how the business benefits, aligned with its long-term strategy, in addition to the societal benefits.
- Explore opportunities for capacity building through Employee Engagement programs. Meet with Human Resources of a potential corporate sponsor. How might these "knowledge workers" support your nonprofit while contributing in a meaningful way?
- Identify natural affinities between your cause and a brand? Where do you donors shop? Does your "donor base" have shared interest with a company's "customer base?"
- Seek out CEO's for your board or create an "Advisory Board."
- Identify crowdsourcing opportunities between your cause, supporters and corporate partner. How might you leverage a corporate gift with donors?

From the company's perspective:

- As a corporation, learn what cause matters to your customers. Use social media or crowd sourcing to engage with customers and cause.
- Might a portion of every sale contribute to a nonprofit?
- Appoint a Board Member to oversee a company's philanthropic efforts.
- Participate in the "Employee Impact Platform" and create a "Cause Integration Profile" on Causecast.

Collaboration

- Analyze your organization's individual contribution and place within the whole puzzle. What type of collaboration aligns well with your cause?

- Make a list of other nonprofits that work within your similar or adjacent space by asking, "Who wins when we win." Build a coalition around shared values while defining your self-interest within it.
- Find partner organizations for funding opportunities from a foundation, especially for training and technology grants.
- Share data, retreat themes, webinars and research studies across an issue to better maximize resources.
- Utilize Chaperoned messaging to build online reach.
- Explore opportunities to provide a service or product on behalf of a federal program.
- Add "Super-connectors" to your board.
- To allow the best ideas to surface, how might your organization build in more collaboration in your programs? Is there a partner agency who might co-create a program?

Resources for Corporate Philanthropy and Collaboration

"Rethinking Corporate Giving: Western Union's CEO Offers Her Philosophy," by Caroline Preston, June 3, 2010, The Chronicle of Philanthropy, http://philanthropy.com/article/Rethinking-Corporate-Giving-/65794/

"How To Find and Keep Business Partners," Cause Marketing Forum, Cause Marketing 101 http://www.causemarketingforum.com/site/c.bkLUKcOTLkK4E/b.6 441545/k.7DAD/Business_Partners_for_NPOs.htm

"When Innovation meets Social Good, Consumers Win," by Shawn Paar, December 1, 2011, Fast Company; http://www.fastcompany.com/1798513/when-innovation-meets-social-good-consumers-win

"Cause Marketing: Finding Opportunities In Objectives," 06/28/2011, The Nonprofit Times, http://www.thenonprofittimes.com/article/detail/cause-marketing-finding-opportunities-in-objectives-3936

"15 Ways To Power Cause Marketing Partnerships," Nonprofit Times, 10/05/2011; http://www.thenonprofittimes.com/article/detail/15-ways-to-power-cause-marketing-partnerships-4117

"Needle-Moving Community Collaboratives: A promising Approach to Achieving America's Biggest Challenges," by Willa Seldon, February 6, 2012. http://www.bridgespan.org/needle-moving-community-collaboratives.aspx

Websites for Corporate Philanthropy and Collaboration

Causecast – Employee Engagement programs - http://causecast.com/

Global Giving – http://www.globalgiving.org/corporate-partners/services

(5) Fundraising

- Review your fundraising campaigns. Are the goals clearly tied to program impact? Do donors perceive the impact of their gifts towards achieving a goal?
- How might your organization utilize Peer-to-Peer Fundraising Campaigns? Determine how social media will support these campaigns, especially in maximizing a volunteer's self-interest.
- Examine you volunteer base. Are there volunteers who might be willing to support your fundraising efforts?
- Develop a Monthly Sustainer program. What specifically could this program fund? How might it excite the donor?
- Establish clear metrics of online campaigns. What are the questions used to assure campaign results?
- Do your online campaigns include different "landing pages" for different types of donors?
- Identify a timely issue for a specific appeal. Using a large e-mail list, establish a true deadline and "Call to Action" to solicit funds with urgency.
- Create a Referral program. Ask current supporters to bring in new donors.
- Design specific relationship building plans for Major Donors and new prospects.

Resources for Fundraising

"Building an Effective Email List," by Jay Leslie, Third Sector New England, Boston, MA,
http://www.tsne.org/site/c.ghLUK3PCLoF/b.7885057/k.9A51/Articl es_Building_an_Effective_Email_List_for_Your_Nonprofit.htm

"Raise More By Avoiding One Size Fits All Email Appeals," by Mike Snusz, November 29th, 2011;
http://www.netwitsthinktank.com/marketing-and-communication/raise-more-by-avoiding-one-size-fits-all-email-appeals.htm

"Ten Common Mistakes in Selecting Donor Databases (And How to Avoid Them)," by Robert Weiner, February, 2012;

(http://www.idealware.org/articles/ten_common_mistakes_in_selecti
ng_donor_databases.php)

"A Few Good Tools for Friend-to-Friend Fundraising," by Andrea
Berry and Stella Hernandez, July, 2011:
http://idealware.org/FGTOnlineDistributedFundraising.php

"44 Ways to Turn Your Supporters into Fundraising Superstars,"
posted by Mike Snusz May 25th, 2011:
http://www.netwitsthinktank.com/friends-asking-friends/44-ways-
to-turn-your-supporters-into-fundraising-superstars.htm

(6) Donor Loyalty

- Examine your relationships with different supporters: is the focus "donor-centered" versus overly centered on the transaction? Do you understand the donor's intent and motivations for giving?
- Implement a Communications Calendar for (1) building momentum in your fundraising, (2) engaging donors during campaigns, (3) thanking donors and (4) building community.
  - o Communicate clear specifics about what funds support, at a level that is meaningful to the donor.
  - o Let donors experience the thermometer movement.
  - o Ask for input without solicitation through social media conversations.
- Design a clear recognition program for all level of gifts that is personal, timely and sincere.
  - o Create video, audio tracks and e-mails with compelling human stories to express gratitude.
  - o Send a sincere and prompt thank you, signed by a top person in the organization immediately after a donation.
  - o Clarify specific reasons why a current donor should give again.

Resources for Donor Loyalty

11 Ways To Use Technology To Thank Your Donors, by Andrea Berry and Chris Bernard, August, 2011
http://idealware.org/articles/11-ways-thank-donors-technology

(7) Additional Sustainable Practices

- Make sure your organization has a clear internal and external identity.
- Update your strategic plan, and review it quarterly.
- Offer a product or service and or develop alternative sources of revenue.
- Take action to continually strengthen the board and staff. Identify what will attract potential employees and volunteers to your organization? Provide educational opportunities for your staff and Executive Director.
- Conduct an outside financial audit.
- List board members prominently.

Resources for Additional Sustainable Practices

Why you Need to Game Your Supporters, by Frank Barry, September 13th, 2011; Netwits Thinktank, Blackbaud; http://www.netwitsthinktank.com/gaming/why-you-need-to-game-your-supporters.htm

Venture Forth!: The Essential Guide to Starting a Moneymaking Business in Your Nonprofit Organization, Rolfe Larson April 1, 2002 Fieldstone Alliance

Generating and Sustaining Nonprofit Earned Income: A Guide to Successful Enterprise Strategies, Sharon M. Oster, Cynthia W. Massarsky,Samantha L. Beinhacker, Jossey-Bass, April 26, 2004

Revenue Sources

"Mouse Clicks for Cash: Supporting Nonprofits through Online Retail," by Chris Bernard, January, 2012: http://idealware.org/articles/mouse-clicks-cash-supporting-nonprofits-through-online-retail

Strategic Planning and Leadership

Why Do You Do What You Do? Free-range Thinking Monthly Journal, 2008, Andy Goodman; http://www.agoodmanonline.com/newsletter/archive_2008.htm

The Executive Director's GUIDE to Thriving as a Nonprofit Leader, 2nd Edition by Mim Carlson and Margaret Donahue (The Jossey-Bass Nonprofit Guidebook Series), April 26, 2010

Strategic Planning for Public and Nonprofit Organizations: A Guide to Strengthening and Sustaining Organizational Achievement, 4th Edition, John M. Bryson (The Jossey-Bass Nonprofit Guidebook Series) July 2011

Boards That Make a Difference: A New Design for Leadership in Nonprofit and Public Organizations, 3rd Edition [E-Book] Th*e Jossey-Bass Nonprofit Guidebook Series* by John Carver, E-Book, March 2011

Boosting Board Collaboration: Software to Support Your Board, by Chris Bernard, Senior Editor, March, 2011; http://www.idealware.org/articles/boosting-board-collaboration-software-support-your-board

Conclusion

Imagine for a moment, achieving or sustaining your organization's mission. Your donors do this every time they write a check or make a pledge. It is equally important that you and everybody in the organization embrace sustainability as well.

On a professional level, how would it feel to attend a training conference, unaffordable last year? How about working on a new computer at the office and an iPad when in the field? Wouldn't you feel excited at the prospect of hiring an assistant? Increasing your budget for outreach? Operating from a place of financial strength would drastically shift a nonprofit's potential.

Envision the application of modern fundraising practices, combining innovation and reinvented fundamentals, to achieve financial sustainability for your organization. Dream about the ensuing possibilities.

Admittedly, it's difficult to imagine success when much uncertainty still exists in our world, negatively affecting charitable giving. Donations continue to lag behind 2007 levels and many nonprofits operate on budgets with fewer receipts than available five years ago. Shifting demographics and new technology create additional challenges.

Yet as we learned from the leaders in this book, the current landscape is full of opportunity. In their interviews, these experts show us how to reinvent fundraising fundamentals, champion corporate philanthropy and collaboration, integrate marketing and leverage technology. They demonstrate how modern fundraising positively impacts Strategic Planning, Marketing, Donor Loyalty and Board Management. The leaders in this book are innovators seeking to reinvent fundamentals and utilize current- new-innovative resources to solve problems. They are *Fundraising Innovators*.

It's possible for you, too, the fundraiser, to accomplish the same success. If a modern approach is applied strategically, donations will increase, resources will be better maximized, and financial sustainability might become more common, ultimately, helping nonprofits achieve their missions. Increased engagement might also occur between the for-profit company, the social entrepreneur and the nonprofit, exchanging and embracing applicable components of each other's practices.

At the center of fundraising is the individual donor who wants change for the better. The interviewees remind us that it's our job to reach these many generous souls and help them make the logical connection to our cause, whether through traditional means of communication or technology. Focusing on the individual and a contemporary approach are key. While technology will be a big enabler, the experts in *Fundraising Innovators* affirm that we must work efficiently, create partnerships, and inspire others to become involved "in the good fight."

Bonus Interview: John Shaw: Corporate Leaders as the Face of Philanthropy

"There's an old saying: what you give comes back to you tenfold, and in my life, it's come back one-hundred fold."

-John Shaw, Chairman of Jefferies Family Scholarship, 2002-2007

Themes
Organizational Structure, Strategic Planning, Corporate Philanthropy, Fundraising Strategies, Behavioral Economics

Profile
Nonprofit Experience: Jefferies Family Scholarship, St. Francis High School, St. Joan of Arc grammar school, Education and Hope, Ability First, AMVETS, Levitt Pavilion, Special Olympics, Westport Play House

Business Experience: Jefferies Company, 1983-2002, National Sales Manager to President

Mission: "The Jefferies Family Scholarship provides both meritorious recognition and monetary assistance for the education of children of Jefferies employees. Significant scholarships go to the most worthy students with financial need who have demonstrated a passion and commitment to attaining their full potential through academic achievement or perseverance in the face of adversity. The program also presents the Jefferies Award of Merit to those without financial need who have demonstrated the same qualities."

Background

Education has been John's main philanthropic focus. Admiring its founder, Boyd Jeffery, John Shaw was involved with the Jefferies Family Scholarship almost since the inception. Initially Boyd Jeffery donated his own money in addition to support from friends and family. Five years later, when John Shaw became Chair of the

Jefferies Family Scholarship, he raised its profile, setting the goal of raising a million dollars, every year.

By federal law, only 25% of the applicants can receive a scholarship. John set the dual goals of increasing applications for the scholarship and thus the ability to increase the amount of money awarded.

In his interview, John shares with us the importance and power of building a large network of supporters. He also explains why corporate philanthropy benefits a company's bottom line, and, how, as a fundraiser, to leverage this type of partnership. He espouses classic fundraising tools that have a proven track record. His material strengthens fundamentals.

Interview

Please tell me how the Jefferies Family Scholarship program has raised money. Which fundraising vehicles have been the most successful?
Our biggest fundraiser was a high-end raffle. Tickets were always $100 each and employees, especially those whose children had benefitted from a scholarship, not only donated prizes but also sold tickets, both within and outside of the firm. Prizes included exotic vacations and shares of Jefferies stock. At one sales meeting, we raised over a million dollars.

Another vehicle for raising money was straight solicitations, made mainly from officers on the JFS board. We, board members, made donations ourselves and also solicited other employees for larger gifts, especially from those employees with close ties to the company's founder or people who had been identified with the scholarship over a long period of time. When I asked for donations, I also leveraged my position and the networks I had created when I served as National Sales Manager and then as President.

Another source of funds came from the company itself. Jefferies Companies felt that it was a good policy to offer scholarships to family members. I even used the scholarship opportunity as a recruiting tool for potential employees.

What are the absolute basics that must be in place before any organization can successfully fundraise for a cause?

Naturally, you need a clear cause. Then you must create an army composed of people who believe in the cause and are willing to work towards your goals. As the leader of the army, you must network. Instead of just fifteen "Believers" selling raffle tickets, you also engage fifteen "Lieutenants" who build their own armies and each recruit ten additional sellers, creating a team of one hundred and sixty five members.

How would someone who does not feel well "networked" create an army?

Find people who have built a strong reputation in the community and already have armies of their own. Also, ask the question: Who else might benefit from supporting this cause? When raising $5 million to build a new Catholic high school, I approached the Bishop of Joliet and asked him to make a leading gift of $250,000. At that time, this bishop had a reputation of closing secondary schools. Knowing that the diocese had made such a large commitment to a new high school, other donors followed. The Bishop's generous donation also immensely improved his standing in the community.

Are there business disciplines that should be incorporated into fundraising? Why or why not?

In order to be successful in business, it's necessary to have a plan and then execute that plan with discipline. Fundraising is similar but you also need a clear cause and, of course, an army of people to market and spread the word about the cause.

When you examine the nonprofit sector, what causes do the best job of differentiating themselves and why?

Special Olympics does the best job. They not only have a clear cause, but repeatedly demonstrate their results, mainly through their eye-catching posters. Vivid client pictures on the posters illustrate the benefit of donor dollars in advancing the mental, physical and spiritual well being of the Special Olympic beneficiaries.

AMVETS is another organization that is very effective in fundraising. Their callers contact past donors and are persistent, yet don't hound people. Callers sincerely tell the true stories of injured American soldiers returning home and struggling with personal and family needs. Heartstrings are pulled and it's hard to resist making a donation.

Do you have a sense that there is an 80-20 rule in fundraising?
Generally an 80/20 rule applies, because the top 20% of donors have the ability to give. The remaining 80% are benevolent, too, but they just don't have the resources to write big checks. The rule I follow, however, is more like 2/18/80. The top 2% can provide the most money in a campaign.

What do you think is key to generating loyal donor relationships?
Although people move on in their support of different causes, perhaps choosing four per year, like me, loyalty nevertheless attaches itself to a clear cause. When you have loyal donors, seize on the opportunity and ask them for a contribution again the following year. Donors will expect to be solicited a second, third, and even a fourth time, putting charitable dollars aside each year in anticipation of being asked. And it's their right to say "No." Be careful to ask for enough, but not too much. When soliciting for a repeat donation, push up "The Ask."

How should corporations support philanthropy?
People are proud to work at a place that is generous. When the company helps others, employees feel good. I think employees who make large salaries are instinctively generous. At a brokerage firm like Jefferies, the brokers are the best givers in the world!

For employees to feel comfortable engaging in philanthropy, a company must offer a benevolent environment. For example, at Jefferies, all employees receive stock every year, as well as family members having access to the Jefferies Family Scholarships.

Philanthropy at Jefferies also has "faces" which are represented by people who are valued and respected within the company. These employees carry the charitable banner forward and epitomize management's commitment to "doing good." A corporation's management team can either enhance or ruin this commitment. Some companies respond to solicitation by saying: "We can't give any corporate money because it belongs to the shareholders."

How do you respond to this potential conflict between charity and stockholders?
I believe that shareholders, if ever asked, would never reject thoughtful corporate giving, because such gifts do not adversely

affect the stock price. The contrary is true as well, since charitable donations enhance the perceived value of a company. After I handed Bill Clinton a check for seven million dollars to benefit 9/11 charities, he recognized the Jefferies Company nine months later in a speech he gave at the Ahmanson Theater in Los Angeles. Such recognition added tremendous value to Jefferies as a public company, even indirectly creating new stockholders who invested because they were aware of our benevolence.

Have you seen any successful collaborations between nonprofits sharing a similar mission?
The Catholic church in my area collaborates with the founder of Education and Hope, an orphanage and school in Guatemala. Aligning with the values and outreach of the Catholic Church, the founder is allowed to solicit parishes on behalf of the orphanage. Overall, however, I have not seen much collaboration between nonprofits.

What do you know now as a leader that you wish you had known sooner?
Maximize your corporate leadership especially for the philanthropic space. When you're in a position of power, your ability to "get things done" is enhanced. I'm not advocating soliciting by intimidation; rather as a leader, you have a platform to persuade and lead other employees to support a cause.

How might nonprofits move to a new level of resilience?
In fundraising, consistent solicitation is key. Every month, I receive an invitation, or a raffle ticket, or something, from Covenant House, a women's shelter in New York City. They have a highly organized, original fundraising calendar. Inevitably, I purchase or donate at some point during the year, maybe even more than once.

How have technology and social media changed fundraising and how might organizations maximize these opportunities?
Although many people do not want to be solicited on the Internet, in fact, offering multiple points of solicitation is best. The more places you can touch a donor, the more success you will have. Actor Danny Thomas and his daughter, actress Marlo Thomas have elevated the use of television and magazines for St Jude's Children's Hospital. Radio personality Don Imus has repeatedly donated the

use of his ranch to help kids who have terminal cancer. Using the airwaves and social media and then linking these spokespersons to personal contact creates a winning strategy.

Discoveries

- To successfully fundraise for a cause, you need a network or "army of believers" who are willing to work towards achieving financial goals and market the cause; fifteen "Believers" who recruit fifteen "Lieutenants" who create additional armies, recruiting ten sellers each.
- Classic fundraising tools work: such as a high-end raffle, direct solicitation of the Board and its referral networks.
- In large campaigns, it's possible that the giving ratio is 2/18/80 with two percent providing the majority of funds.
- Philanthropy supports a corporation's business because (1) employees are proud to work at a company that is generous; (2) those that earn large salaries are inherently generous; (3) the perceived value of a company is enhanced by thoughtful charitable giving and does not adversely affect its stock price. The management team should represent the philanthropic face of a company.

Key Take Aways

- Leverage the position of a corporate executive for fundraising and raising awareness around a cause. Recognize that a leader has a platform to persuade and lead other employees to support a cause.
- To create an initial group of supporters ask "Who might benefit from our cause."
- When you have loyal donors, seize on the opportunity to ask them again the following year after year. They will expect to be asked again.
- When reaching out to donors, especially on the phone, be sincere and relate an emotional story that is personal and pulls heartstrings.

Acknowledgements

I would like to thank my sweetheart husband, Jay, who has been steadfast in his support of this writing project. I could not have married a more thoughtful man. My children, too, Kaelyn and Henry, have been excited for me. Thank you.

This book would not be possible without the many leaders who generously gave their wisdom and energy to an interview in this book. Their knowledge about fundraising and giving form the foundation of *Fundraising Innovators*. I'm extremely grateful for their willingness to share their wisdom and stories with me. A big "Wow" and "Thank You" for their generosity! It's very affirming.

I would also like to thank Brian Schwartz, my publisher, who is always encouraging, extremely patient and positive.

In 1982, my parents, Hank and Charlotte Stifel, formed a foundation to fund spinal cord paralysis research, motivated to cure my brother, Henry. Their leadership has been pivotal in so many ways. Since his accident thirty years ago, Henry, has continued to lead and inspire others not only in the field of cure research but in his workplace and community. My sisters, Stephanie and Wendy, have also never ceased in their efforts to contribute to the Christopher and Dana Reeve Foundation. I have been truly lucky to have a loving family of "do-ers" motivated to make things better.

There's an extensive list of enthusiasts who have helped me. I would also like to acknowledge the following people for their support and or contribution in some way: Lynn Tetrault, Mary Dooley, Kris Kerr, Colleen Kennedy, Tami Lacks and the Colorado Chapter of AFP "Coffee Chat" participants, Marie Picasso, Don McGrath, Maribeth Bowen, the many "Readers," Paul Luber, Jim Bolt, the Tech4Good Advisory Board, Francine Mathews, Darci Davenport, Michael Doyle, Steve Heye, Mimi Cook, Jackie Hawkey, Martha Tracey, Donna Krone, John Abraham, Shanna Belott (who totally "Saved the Day" for me), my "Title" judges via e-mail, On Broadway Toastmasters, Kathryn Harris, Tina Drum, Tom Howard, Regina and Robert deWetter…
Thank you for being a part of this exciting project!

About The Author

Amy Quinn is an author, fundraiser, and volunteer who seeks to build community by engaging friends and acquaintances in support of local and national nonprofits. As a fundraiser, she's motivated to help organizations raise the necessary funds to achieve their respective missions.

Prior to writing this book, Amy has held a variety of nonprofit leadership roles as well as initiated several community projects. She is especially passionate about medical research to cure spinal cord paralysis.

Amy holds a Masters in Business Administration from Thunderbird School of Global Management and her BA from Bucknell University and enjoys public speaking as a hobby.

Stay in touch with Amy online at:

www.FundraisingInnovators.com

http://www.Facebook.com/FundraisingResources

Appendix A: 18 Leadership Principles of Nonprofit Leaders

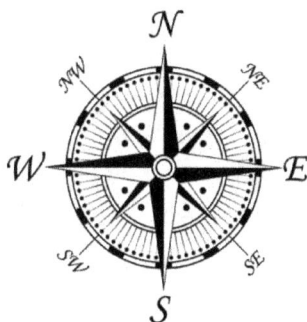

One of my favorite questions occurred towards the end of almost every interview:

What do you know now as a leader that you wish you had known sooner?

Usually the interviewee briefly paused and then responded; strong leaders reflect on what they've learned. Since leadership affects fundraising, I've summarized the responses below as a soothing and logical book-end to this book. I hope that you will feel motivated and inspired by these leadership principles.

1. **Listen.** Listen is central to leading. Hear what your employees, partners and constituents say (Holly Ross).

2. **Ask.** Although planning is essential, at the end of the day, you have to ask people to donate (Holly Ross).

3. **Act on what you say you're going to do** (Eric Scroggins).

4. **Excellence matters.** Completing the task correctly is a motivational tool because often people do not follow through (Eric Scroggins).

5. **Balance Passion and Business Enterprise.** There needs to be a balance in equal measure between passion and business enterprise (Peter Kiernan).

6. **Super-connect.** Leaders are "super-connectors;" people who mentor, collaborate, inspire, give back, speak at panels, raise their hand and show up (Rich Rainaldi).

7. **Pursue your joy**. The more you **"pursue your joy"** the more success you'll have (Richard Crespin).

8. **Make a Contribution to Others versus Solely Serving Your Self.** To find your purpose, identify what you care about. The "great reward" then comes through serving others rather than solely serving yourself (Simon Mainwaring).

9. **Experiment.** It's good to be somewhat naive about challenges you might face and instead just keep experimenting with different scenarios and solutions and then eliminate the processes that don't work (Ryan Scott).

10. **Demonstrate Why Your Cause Matters.** It's important to demonstrate why what you're doing matters to others. Relationship building and proving personal relevance are continual exercise in fundraising (Katya Andresen).

11. **Ground your work from a place of abundance versus extraction.** Fundraising is the business of happiness. It is not the practice of extracting money. Fundraising provides an opportunity for people to make an amazing change in the world through their gifts. The emotional ROI (Return on Investment) is far above any retail therapy. We can be far more successful when we ground our work from a place of abundance versus simply focusing on our own need (Katya Andresen).

12. **Nonprofit practices overlap for-profit practices.** Successful nonprofits follow business principles while understanding that profits represent societal benefits for the greater good (Henry G. Stifel).

13. **Maximize corporate leadership.** Maximize your corporate leadership position especially for the philanthropic space. When you're in a position of power, your ability to "get things done" is enhanced. I'm not advocating soliciting by

intimidation; rather, as a leader, you have a platform to persuade and lead other employees to support a cause (John Shaw).

14. **Trust Your Gut and Be Willing to Take Risks.** Being too cautious might have saved me from making mistakes, but it also might have kept me from achieving some really important victories (Scott Daigneault).

15. **Give Back To Others.** Collaborate to build success for not only your organization but for others. Don't ignore self-interest in a collaborative but aspire to give back to others, too (Francisco Gonima).

16. **Understand the life stage of your organization.** Understanding the life stage of your organization will facilitate a quicker process to reaching goals (Peter Wilderotter).

17. **Succeed at the grass-roots level of the organization.** The success of an organization is determined by what occurs at the grass-roots level. Front line workers need to feel passionate, empowered and knowledgeable and aligned in terms of standards of operation and a company's goals (Vinay Bhagat).

18. **Appreciate the relationship, people-side of the business.** To gain "Shower time" focus on the proper incentive structure for employees to go "the extra mile." "Shower time" is when an employee is so motivated that they have crisp moments of problem solving during "off hours" (Ed Messman).

Appendix B: Index of Nonprofits, Public/Private Partnerships, Social Entrepreneurships and Corporate Foundations

Ability First Bank Aquillo
American Cancer Society
Amnesty International
American Red Cross
American Veterans of World War II (AMVETS)
Architecture For Humanity
Avaaz
A Wider Circle
The Brooklyn Community Foundation
Causecast
Charity Water
CiviCore
The Children's Hospital Foundation
Christopher and Dana Reeve Foundation
Colorado I Have a Dream Foundation
Colorado Nonprofit Association
Colorado Planned Giving Roundtable
Convio
Corporate Responsibility Magazine
Corporate Responsibility Officer's Association
Covenant House (NYC)
Crowdrise
The Darden School of Business
Denver Public Schools Foundation
Denver Scientific and Cultural Facilities District
DonorsChoose
Education and Hope
Epic Change
Friends of Island
Giveo
Google

Global Brand Initiative (GBI)
Huffington Post
The Humane Society
IBM Foundation
IBM Smarter Planet
Invisible Children
The Jefferies Family Scholarship Foundation
The Kessler Foundation
The Levitt Pavilion
Let's Move Initiative
Live Strong Foundation
The Massaii Wilderness Conservation Trust
The Miami Project
The Michigan Land Use Institute
The Michael J. Fox Foundation for Parkinson's Research
The Mississippi Valley Conservancy
M & R Consulting Services
National Committee on Planned Giving
The National Jewish Health Foundation
The National Museum of Wildlife Art
National Organization of Rare Diseases
Nike's Green Exchange
The Nature Conservancy
Network for Good
The Nielsen Foundation
The Nonprofit Technology Network (NTEN)
Planned Parenthood of the Rocky Mountains
Product Red
Rebuilding Together USA
Robinhood Foundation
Socialvest
St. Judes Children's Hospital
St. Vincent's Hospital (Westchester, NY)
Salesforce
Special Olympics
The Sharpe Group
Start Up America Partnership
Summer Scholars
Teach For America
TechSoup

Theodore Roosevelt Conservation Partnership
Trout Unlimited
UNICEF
Union Sportsmen Alliance
The United Way
University of Denver
Urban Peak
Verizon Wireless Foundation
Vero Beach Art Museum
We First
Wells Fargo Foundation
Westport Playhouse
Yellow Dog Watershed Preserve

Appendix C: Case Study - Let the Shoe Fit: Zappos and Online Development

How many people have ever donated online? Bought shoes from Zappos? I'm a big fan of both! One day in 1999, founder of Zappos, Nick Swinmurn, was shopping for a pair of shoes in San Francisco. Either the store did not have the right size, color nor style and he went home empty-handed. This experience led Swinmurn to quit his day job and start an online shoe business!!

There were "naysayers" that said.... "No, No, No, people won't buy shoes online. They don't buy shoes that way. They have to see and feel the shoes." It's now 2012, thirteen years later and Zappos' gross sales are in the billions. It has built an outstanding reputation for customer service, 24/7, 365 days a year, in addition to free shipping always, on all orders, both directions!

Similarly there are "naysayers" who contend online fundraising can only go so far. "There's not enough personal contact. E-mail is so impersonal and donors need to be touched." Through research and the interviews in this book, we have learned that it is possible to touch a donor, broaden reach and community and raise money online! The average online donation is $100 versus $30 for direct mail. As documented in the research paper, "The Wired Wealthy," there are already a significant number of large online donations, defined as $5000 or more. But it's not just about the money. Online development is much bigger than that.

Let's examine shifting the perspective around online fundraising like Zappos shifted the paradigm around buying shoes.

Quick Delivery

Zappos believes that the speed in which a customer receives an online order affects whether that shopper will shop their site again. It does everything possible to deliver quickly.

Online communication, including fundraising, offers speed, low cost and multiple channels, 24/7, 365 days. A nonprofit can be immediately transparent in all actions and results.

The Right Shoe

Zappos never offers an item for sale if it is not already in its warehouse; that's integrity and for practical reasons is the only way to have quick delivery. Zappos warehouses more than three million items for any individual.

No matter how many contributors, it's also possible to be able to deliver the "right shoe;" the right message online. If you sign up for information about cats at The Humane Society website, you will never receive information about dogs! If you segment your donors, the "shoe" can fit perfectly online!

An Emotional Connection

According to their core values at Zappos, a key ingredient in strong relationships is to develop emotional connections with customers. The same can be said about donors. Donors, especially Baby Boomers, want to feel the impact of their gift. They want to know why it matters. As Katya Andresen illustrated in her interview, using A Wider Circle as an example, it is possible to create an emotional connection with a donor. If organizations tell their stories well, donors feel compelled to give.

Gratitude and integrity

At Zappos it's "important to make sure that you do the right thing and treat your relationships well." How might you treat your donors well online?

It's very simple. Gratitude. Again Katya Andresen asserts that technology is uniquely suited to deepen human relationships over time. In addition to sending thoughtful e-mails, which cost pennies, watching a video we can vividly see the impact of a donation. We can listen and experience an interview with individuals who are benefitting from a gift.

206

Engagement

Social media is about joining conversations that already exist. It's about a nonprofit locating people who have a natural affinity for its cause and understanding where to congregate, listen and interact with those followers online. It's NOT just about asking for money! The potential to engage at a new and inspiring level is huge. Go ahead...ask your donors for input on your next project!

Conclusion

Zappos hopes that one day it will capture 30% of all online shoe purchases. The online shoe business represents 40 billion in revenue. In charitable giving 294 million was donated to charities in 2010. Of that, over 70% was donated by individuals. If you add in 10% of donations in the form of bequests, the individual percentage of total donations is over 80% of 294 million. How much might online donations capture one day?

While Major Donors need special attention and will continue, in the short term, to provide the highest total donation percentage, it would be a terrible mistake not to develop broader reach; build friends, followers, fans and key online influencers. Engage. Outreach does not have to be only about asking for money.

Even if the percentage of online donations at your organization is small today, it can grow with cultivating and engaging individuals in a variety of ways. Obviously expanding your online presence will allow you to reach younger donors too, in addition to Baby Boomers who donate and engage more and more online. Loyalty over time, building a base (a large base) impacts a nonprofit's sustainability. Small loyal donors often become your larger donors.

Success online is not yet universal, nor is it even a best practice; but this is changing. Utilize varied online engagement, demonstrate gratitude, and deliver current results immediately with integrity, and transparency. Make an emotional connection through telling your stories. By doing this, your organization will deliver the "right shoe and fit". It's time to "let the shoe drop" and embrace the potential of online development!

Appendix D: Additional Resources

Community: The Structure of Belonging by Peter Block; Berrett-Koehler Publishers Inc., 2008, 2009

Donor Centered Fundraising: How to Hold on to Your Donors and Raise Much More Money by Penelope Burk (recommended by Scott R. Lumpkin, Vice Chancellor, University of Denver, University Advancement)

Effective Fundraising for Nonprofits: Real-World Strategies That Work by Ilona Bray, J.D. ; NOLO, third edition, August 2010

Family Wealth- Keeping it in the Family: How Family Members and their Advisers Preserve Human, Intellectual, and Financial Assets for Generations, by James E. Hughes (recommended by Scott R. Lumpkin, Vice Chancellor, University of Denver, University Advancement)

In the context of understanding the origins of poverty, Fish, Stick, Knife, Gun: A Personal History of Violence by Geoffrey Canada

Forces For Good: The Six Practices of High-Impact Nonprofits by Leslie R. Crutchfield and Heather McLeod Grant

Good to Great: Why Some Companies Make the Leap and Others Don't by Jim Collins; HarperCollins Publishing, 2001

Leadership by Rudolph W. Guiliani; Miramax Books, New York, 2002

Little Bets: How Breakthrough Ideas Emerge From Small Discoveries by Peter Sims; Free Press, division of Simon & Schuster, 2011

Managing Technology to Meet Your Mission: A Strategic Guile for Nonprofit Leaders; edited by Holly Ross, Katrin Verclas and Alison Levine; published by NTEN and a variety of authors, 2009.

The Millionaire Next Door: Surprising Secrets of America's Wealthy by Thomas Stanley and William Danko

The Networked Nonprofit: Connecting with Social Media to Drive Change by Beth Kanter and Allison H. Fine, June, 2010

Robin Hood Marketing: Stealing Corporate Savvy to Sell Just Causes by Katya Andresen

The Seven Faces of Philanthropy: A New Approach to Cultivating Major Donor JOSSEY-BASS NONPROFIT & PUBLIC MANAGEMENT SERIES (recommended by Peter Wilderotter, CEO, The Christopher and Dana Reeve Foundation)

The Tipping Point: How Little Things Can Make a Big Difference by Malcolm Gladwell; Little Brown & Company, 2000, 2002

We First; How Brands and Consumers Use Social Media to Build a Better World by Simon Mainwaring; Palgrave Macmillan, a division of St. Martin's Press, 2011

Blogs/Wiki's

Craig C. Wruck, "The Plain English Planned Giving Wiki," http://plannedgifts.wiki.zoho.com/HomePage.html

Katya Andresen's Nonprofit Marketing Blog:http://www.nonprofitmarketingblog.com/

Beth Kantor's, author of The Networked Nonprofit, blog: http://www.bethkanter.org/

Simon Mainwaring's, author and consultant, We First, blog: http://simonmainwaring.com/

Nonprofit Technology Network blog: http://www.nten.org/blog

Helpful Organization Websites

Association of Fundraising Professionals: http://www.afpnet.org/

Alliance Online: http://www.allianceonline.org/

Cause Marketing Forum: www.causemarketingforum.com

Colorado Planned Giving Roundtable: http://www.cpgr.org/

Foundation Center: http://foundationcenter.org/marketplace/catalog/product_directory.jhtml?id=prod10009

The Chronicles of Philanthropy:
http://philanthropy.com/section/Home/172

Pitch Consulting Services:
http://pitchconsulting.blogspot.com/search/label/dan%20heath

Donor Walls; Donor Recognition; Planned
legacyhttp://www.plannedlegacy.com/about-plannedlegacy.html

Grassroots Institute for Fundraising Training:
http://www.grassrootsfundraising.org

Research Reports and Articles

A worthwhile read for understanding e-mail marketing and
fundraising: "2010 eNonprofit Benchmark Study," published by the
Nonprofit Technology Network." http://www.e-
benchmarksstudy.com/

Current information on the impact of Social Media on nonprofit
marketing and fundraising, published by the Nonprofit Technology
Network: "2011 Nonprofit Social Network Benchmark Report"
(http://nonprofitsocialnetworksurvey.com/download.php)

"Storytelling and the Art of Email Writing" by Steve Daigneault
and Colin Holtz; 2011 M+R Strategic Services;
http://labs.mrss.com/storytelling-and-the-art-of-email-writing/

"Does Social Responsibility Help Protect a Company's Reputation?"
by Andreas B. Eisingerich and Gunjan Bhardwaj; MIT Sloan
Management Review, March, 2011; http://sloanreview.mit.edu/the-
magazine/2011-spring/52313/does-social-responsibility-help-
protect-a-companys-reputation/

"The Impact of Cause Integration" by Ryan Scott, Founder,
Causecast, May 13th, 2011; http://causecast.org/blog/csr/impact-
cause-integration

"The 2011 Online Giving Report" by Steve MacLaughline, Jim
O'Shaughnessy and Allison Van Diest; February, 2012, Blackbaud.

The Money for Good initiative provides a comprehensive
understanding of the behaviors, attitudes, and motivations of affluent
Americans with respect to impact investing, charitable giving, and
210

international entrepreneurship. Their reports have helped me understand the tie between charitable donations and impact investing as well as learning more about the individual motivations for giving. This link connects you to the following reports: http://www.hopeconsulting.us/money-for-good/

"The US Market for Impact Investments and Charitable Gifts from Individual Donors and Investors," May 2010;

"Impact Investing Overview," May 2010;

"Special Report on Donor and Investor Preferences for Supporting Organizations Working Outside the US."

"The Next Generation of American Giving", by Convio and Edge Research, which looks at the effect of multi-channel marketing on different generations; http://www.convio.com/signup/next-generation/next-generation-of-american-giving-whitepaper.html

"Integrated Mulit-Channel Marketing: Where Nonprofit Organizations Are Today & Key Success Factors Moving Forward" by Edge Research adn Convio; authored by Vinay Bhagat, Founder & Chief Strategy Officer, Convio; http://www.convio.com/signup/guides/integrated-multi-channel-marketing/

"Drowning in Data," Stanford Social Innovation Review, by Alana Conner Snibbe, Fall, 2006 http://www.ssireview.org/articles/entry/drowning_in_data

http://www.causemarketingforum.com/site/c.bkLUKcOTLkK4E/b.6 381267/k.B2B8/Cause_Marketing_Forum__Helping_Businesses__ Nonprofits_Succeed_Together.htm

http://foundationcenter.org/marketplace/catalog/product_directory.jh tml?id=prod10009

http://www.fundraisingsuccessmag.com/#utm_source=fundraisingsu ccessmag.com&utm_medium=article_page&utm_campaign=top_na v

http://www.msnbc.msn.com/id/34850532/ns/technology_and_scienc e-wireless/t/mobile-giving-help-haiti-exceeds-million/

http://www.blackbaud.com/files/resources/downloads/WhitePaper_
MultiChannelGivingAnalysis.pdf

http://www.annenbergalchemy.org/resources/2010AlchemyResource
Guide.pdf

http://hbr.org/2011/01/the-big-idea-creating-shared-value/ar/1

http://www.createthefuture.com/Whats%20New.htm

http://seminars.idealware.org/documents/donor_management_workb
ook_v3.pdf

http://www.idealware.org/sites/idealware.org/files/IdealwareDonor
Mgmt2011_0.pdf

http://www.asaecenter.org/Shop/BookstoreDetail.cfm?ItemNumber=
40369

http://philanthropy.com/article/Don-t-Judge-a-Charity-by-
Its/127699/

http://www.fastcompany.com/magazine/157/how-to-train-your-
celebrity

http://www.edelman.com/trust/2011/

http://www.agoodmanonline.com/pdf/bad_ads_high_res/BadAdsHi.
pdf

http://www.agoodmanonline.com/pdf/BadPresentationsHi.pdf

http://www.nten.org/blog/2011/09/21/fourteen-ways-improve-your-
open-
rate?utm_source=ntenconnect&utm_medium=email&utm_content=
other&utm_campaign=sep11

http://www.huffingtonpost.com/craig-newmark/infographic-how-
the-top-5_b_1011176.html?ir=Technology

http://www.idealware.org/facebook_survey

http://www.ssireview.org/articles/entry/creating_high_impact_nonpr
ofits

http://www.grassrootsfundraising.org/why-gift/staff-board/

Care USA; Chaperoned E-mailsL http://www.sofii.org/node/312

http://www.ssireview.org/articles/entry/drowning_in_data

Due Diligence on Nonprofits – Web Site Searches

Charity Navigator: http://www.charitynavigator.org/

Give Well: http://www.givewell.org/

Guide Start: http://www2.guidestar.org/

Great Nonprofits: http://greatnonprofits.org/

Endnotes/Glossary

---

[1] **Sustainability** "is the ability to sustain the work and the impact for as long as there is a need for (the nonprofit). A nonprofit can sustain its work if it can secure the resources it needs, and then put these to best use - use only what is needed and apply them in ways that have the greatest mission effect." Ultimately this book is about raising enough money so a nonprofit can focus on achieving its mission. (http://www.nationalcne.org/index.cfm?fuseaction=feature.display&feature_ID=1 26&CFID=746&CFTOKEN=97183526)

[2] **Executive Director (ED)** is usually the head of the nonprofit with overall responsibilities for the nonprofit's mission, programs and fundraising. The ED reports to the nonprofit's Board of Directors.

[3] **Gift Officers:** Fundraising employees charged with soliciting Major Gift donors and or other types of specific donor groups.

[4] **Social Media** is "online communication channels that facilitate interaction and media distribution between people. Unlike more traditional online channels, social media allows for participation, engagement and real-time feedback on the part of supporters and constituents." ("Going Social: Tapping into Social Media for Nonprofit Success," Convio, 2010).

[5] **Integrated Marketing** is combining and planning offline and online efforts when marketing a cause to various donor groups.

[6] **Metrics:** "Metrics" refer to how something is measured so as to be able to evaluate and analyze the results. It's synonymous with "analytics." In fundraising "metrics" refers to establishing goals and benchmarks for measuring success, whether for a program or specific campaign.

[7] Annual Giving Number for 2010: Giving USA 2011: The Annual Report on Philanthropy for the Year 2010; Giving USA Foundation; Researched and written by The Center on Philanthropy at Indiana University, Giving USA 2011

[8] "Employee Burnout: In Challenging Times, Overstretched Board Members Fight Burnout," by Holly Hall, Chronicles of Philanthropy, http://philanthropy.com/article/Overstretched-Board-Members/129215/

"How to Manage Feelings of Burnout, Chronicles of Philanthropy," by Cody Switzer; July, 2011: http://philanthropy.com/article/How-to-Manage-Feelings-of/128191/

"Burnout, Low Pay May Drive Charity Workers Away, Survey Finds," by Caroline Preston, Chronicles of Philanthropy, March, 2007: http://philanthropy.com/article/Burnout-Low-Pay-May-Drive/55156/

[9] **Major Donors** describe a donor group that makes large donations. Fundraisers create specific personalize plans for soliciting and cultivating relationships with these generous donors. For more information, please see "Three Ways to Identify a Major Donor" by Joanne Fritz, About.com.

[10] Number of Nonprofits: According to the National Center for Charitable Statistics (NCCS), 1,574,674 tax-exempt organizations exist in the US (2009),including 959,698 public, 100,337 private foundations and 514,639 other types of nonprofits: http://nccs.urban.org/statistics/quickfats.cfm.

[11] "The Nonprofit Technology Gap- Myth or Reality?" by Stephanie L. Geller, John Hopkins University, Alan J. Abramson, George Mason University, Erwin de Leon, Urban Institute; The Johns Hopkins Nonprofit Listening Post Project, John Hopkins University, Center for Civil Society Studies; 2010 Lester M. Salamon.

[12] **Platform:** "computing platform includes some sort of hardware architecture and a software framework (including application frameworks), where the combination allows software, particularly application software, to run...A platform might be simply defined as a place to launch software." In online fundraising this refers to the ability to customize particular pages for reaching and interacting with specific constituent groups. (http://en.wikipedia.org/wiki/Computing_platform).

[13] *Managing Technology to Meet Your Mission: A Strategic Guide for Nonprofit Leaders*; Pgs. 11 & 12 "Mission First: Achieving IT Alignment" by Steve Heye; The Nonprofit Technology Network, 2009.

[14] **Baby Boomers:** This population group is born between 1946 and 1964. There are roughly 77 million Baby Boomers in the United States. From a fundraising perspective, Baby Boomers particularly care about transparency and understanding the direct impact of their gifts on a nonprofit. (http://www.bbhq.com/whatsabm.htm).

[15] "New Approaches for Today's Realities" presented by Robert F. Sharpe, Jr., President, The Sharpe Group, November 17th, 2011. Denver, Colorado

[16] **The Great Recession:** Beginning in December, 2007 and peaking in September 2008, a global financial collapse and ensuing recession. Although the "economic" recession ended in July 2009, the term is still often used to explain current hardship (as per Wikipedia).

[17] **Campaign:** A defined time period for raising money or engaging supporters with specific goals and plan of action.

[18] **Crowd Sourcing:** "The act of outsourcing tasks to an undefined, large group of people or community (a 'crowd') through an open call." Wikipedia

216

[19] Pyramid from Edward G. Happ, Global CIO and Head of ISD, International Federation of Red Cross and Red Crescent. For more information: http://eghapp.blogspot.com/

[20] **Build Capacity** refers to building the knowledge base of nonprofit employees within corporate philanthropic programs. This means utilizing "knowledge workers" to train and support nonprofit efforts.

[21] **Software as a Service (Saas):** "A common delivery model for a business application in which software and data are hosted in the Internet cloud and delivered via the Internet to the client" (from Wikipedia).

[22] **Customer Relationship Management (CRM)** software- a robust business technology used in sales-oriented jobs, like fundraising, across sectors and "different verticals", not to be confused with Contact Management software. CRM systems help "track constituents, generate leads, integrate e-mail, automate workflow, support collaboration and offer reporting." (http://www.pcmag.com/article2/0,2817,2391297,00.asp)

[23] **Scale Up** is "the ability to function with different amounts of required work, or to be readily adjusted to do so." (http://en.wikipedia.org/wiki/Scale_up) Bill Clinton believes that solutions already exist to many of the worlds' problems but they need to be taken to scale and or enlarged on a bigger scale.

[24] "The Next Generation of American Giving: A Study on contrasting charitable habits of Generation Y, Generation X, Baby Boomers and Matures," Convio, March 2010

[25] Page 18 *Crossing the Chasm* by Geoffrey is a book which "makes the case that high-tech products require marketing strategies that differ from those in other industries. His chasm theory describes how high-tech products initially sell well, mainly to a technically literate customer base, but then hit a lull as marketing professionals try to cross the chasm to mainstream buyers.." Amazon Review, Amazon.com

[26] "Peer-to-Peer Event Fundraising Benchmark Study: Key Performances Benchmarks for the Six Primary Types of Events;" Convio, October 2010.

[27] **Off the Shelf:** "Off the Shelf" refers to existing technology programs available for purchase, "off the shelf" versus technology that is customized to an organization using a consultant.

[28] "The Wired Wealthy: Using the Internet to Connect with Your Middle and Major Donors" by Convio, Sea Change Strategies and Edge Research; March 24th, 2008

[29] To alleviate poverty, Kiva (http://www.kiva.org/) "empowers people around the world with a $25 loan." Kiva's website and worldwide network of microfinance

217

institutions lets an individual make a loan to another individual around the globe. A field worker vets the project and manages the loan to assure the money is paid back. Then, the donor can offer up the money again and the cycle of giving continues. Since it's founding in 2005, Kiva has had 644, 793 lenders, provided $262 million in loans and had a 98.93% re-payment rate in sixty-one different countries (Data from Kiva website, November, 2011).

[30] DonorsChoose.org is "An online charity connecting you to the classrooms in need." DonorsChoose connects individual donors to individual students for specific projects. Donors know exactly how their money is spent and experience a thank you that connects them directly to the students, feeling the benefit on their gift. As of November 30, 2011, DonorsChoose has raised over $94 million and helped 5,560,380 students. In addition, it has funded 230,308 projects at 50,596 schools.

[31] **Advocacy:** "The act of pleading for, supporting or recommending" (Dictionary.com). A 501.4c organization focuses on advocating for change and must pay taxes.

[32] ARC in Haiti and texting results: (http://www.msnbc.msn.com/id/34850532/ns/technology_and_science-wireless/t/mobile-giving-help-haiti-exceeds-million/

[33] Target Analytics Group: http://www.blackbaud.com/; "2011 donorCentrics Internet and Multichannel Giving Benchmarking Report," by Helen Flannery and Rob Harris, July 2011

[34] **80/20:** The 80/20 Rule assumes that 80% of donations come from 20% of donors in a nonprofit. This ratio can typically be higher like 90/10 or 95/5.

[35] **White Label:** "A White label product or service is produced by one company (the producer) that other companies (the marketers) rebrand to make it appear as if they made it." From Wikipedia (http://en.wikipedia.org/wiki/White-label_product)

[36] **Cause Marketing** "Involves the cooperative efforts of a for-profit business and a nonprofit organization for mutual benefit. It refers to any type of marketing effort on behalf of a charitable cause. Cause marketing is a marketing relationship and does not represent a direct donation to a charity." (http://en.wikipedia.org/wiki/Cause_marketing)

[37] **Digital:** "Involving or relating to the use of computer technology," including the Internet and online capabilities. (http://www.answers.com/topic/digital)

[38] **Friends:** A Facebook friend is someone who is connected to another person through the social networking site of the same name. To help protect Facebook members' privacy, one must make a request through the site to become someone else's Facebook friend. It is then up to him or her to accept or or reject the

Facebook friend request. (http://www.wisegeek.com/what-is-a-facebook-friend.htm)

[39] **Web 2.0:** Post the dot.com collapse, Web 2.0 represents applications that "facilitate participatory information sharing, interoperability, user-centered design and collaboration on the Internet." It has SOA (Service Oriented Architecture) including Feeds, Web Services and Social Media and includes interactions with the end user through blogging, podcasts and wiki's. (http://en.wikipedia.org/wiki/Web_2.0
and http://www.youtube.com/watch?v=0LzQIUANnHc)

[40] "The Next Generation of American Giving: A Study on contrasting charitable habits of Generation Y, Generation X, Baby Boomers and Matures," Convio, March 2010

[41] **Web Widgets:** "An application or a component of an interface, that enables a user to perform a function or access a service." Merriam-Webster Dictionary

[42] "Giving USA 2011; The Annual Report on Philanthropy for the year 2010;" Giving USA Foundation, The Center on Philanthropy at Indiana University.

[43] The Wired Wealthy: Using the Internet to Connect with Your Middle and Major Donors'" by Convio, Sea Change Strategies and Edge Research; March 24th, 2008.

[44] **The Ask:** This term refers to the actual words used in a solicitation: the how and what to say when asking for a gift. The interviewees in this book stress that "The Ask" must be "donor-centered."

[45] **Social Enterprise:** "is an organization that applies business strategies to achieving philanthropic goals. Social enterprises can be structured as a for-profit or nonprofit." (http://en.wikipedia.org/wiki/Social_enterprise)

[46] **Behavioral Economics** is the study of why consumers make buying decisions. Some of the same reasons might apply to why a donor makes a donation.

[47] **Social Sector** "One of several terms created as alternatives to 'nonprofit sector' and 'nongovernmental' sector. The latter are seen as putting an emphasis on what this sector is not, rather than calling attention to its focus on a social mission." Defined by Wikipedia (http://en.wikipedia.org/wiki/Social_sector).

[18] **990 Tax Form:** According to Scott Lumkin, "Charities demonstrate their accountability by reporting their activities on IRS Form 990. Although it can take significant organizational resources to complete, this form is an important tool for assessing a nonprofit's operations." All nonprofits must submit this form annually to the IRS.

[49] "Flywheel to Success," pg 164-165, *Good to Great*, Jim Collins, 2001

[50] "Giving USA 2011; The Annual Report on Philanthropy for the year 2010;" Giving USA Foundation, The Center on Philanthropy at Indiana University; Donations to religious organizations: In 2010, religious organizations received the largest share of all charitable gifts, 35% or $100.63 billion.

[51] High-Impact Non-profits:
(http://www.ssireview.org/articles/entry/creating_high_impact_nonprofits)

In the article "Creating High-Impact Nonprofits," Crutchfield and McLeod provide six practices of "High-Impact Non-profits:"

1. Serve and Advocate
2. Make Markets Work
3. Inspire Evangelists
4. Nurture Nonprofit Networks
5. Master the Art of Adaptation
6. Share Leadership

[52] The Fly Wheel defined: pg 164-165, *Good to Great*, Jim Collins, 2001

[53] Move On: Democracy In Action. MoveOn.org Civic Action is a 501 © organization which "focuses on nonpartisan education and advocacy on important national issues. MoveOn.org Political Action is a federal political committee which primarily helps members elect candidates who reflect our values through a variety of activities aimed at influencing the outcome of the next election. MoveOn.org Political Action and MoveOn.org Civic Action are separate organizations. It's site utilizes volunteer editors who explore and post the progressive videos, images etc…for spreading "important ideas" to "win the message war online." Move On has over 5 million members.

[54] Chaperoned Messaging: As an alternative to renting email lists between organizations, on organization sends out a message on behalf of another. This concept works when the integrity of both organization scan be maintained, without the messaging feeling like spam or intrusive to the recipients. For more information, please see: http://news.gilbert.org/Chaperoning

[55] Online Petitions: "An Internet petition is a form of petition posted on a website. Visitors to the website in question can add their email addresses or names, and after enough "signatures" have been collected, the resulting letter may be delivered to the subject of the petition, usually via e-mail." Verification of signatures need to occur. Avaaz, Change.org are two examples of organizations that utilize petitions to mobilize change. Not everyone agrees that petitions achieve their objectives. From Wikipedia.

[56] Page 78 Personal Tribute/Memorial Pages: Many nonprofits offer Personal Tribute/Memorial pages, which allow someone to fundraise for a cause in honor of a loved one or friend. It's a form of Peer to Peer fundraising. Here are some links

to a few examples: Nami:
http://www.nami.org/Template.cfm?Section=Donate_Online&Template=/Content Management/ContentDisplay.cfm&ContentID=109093; Tennyson Center for children: http://www.childabuse.org/Page.aspx?pid=368.

[57] **White-Washing:** "is a metaphor meaning to gloss over;" censorship. (http://en.wikipedia.org/wiki/Whitewash_(censorship)

[58] **Earmark:** To designate a donation to a specific need: "to set aside for a particular purpose" (Oxford American Dictionary)

[59] "Giving USA 2011; The Annual Report on Philanthropy for the year 2010;" Giving USA Foundation, The Center on Philanthropy at Indiana University

[60] **Corporate Responsibility (CR)** or **Corporate Social Responsibility (CSR)** also known as corporate citizenship, responsible business, sustainable responsible business (SRB), or corporate social performance, is a form of corporate self-regulation integrated into a business model. ...," "the degree to which companies manage business practices to produce an overall positive impact on society," Term used to cover all areas of responsible behavior by companies including ethical behavior, corporate governance and environmental impact." (http://en.wikipedia.org/wiki/Corporate_responsibility; http://www.clevelandcarbonfund.org/resources/sustainability-dictionary/; http://www.itvplc.com/glossaryterm/)

[61] **Russell 1000** Companies represent the top 1000 companies by capitalization that are tracked in an index. "The Russell Indexes are a family of global equity indices that allow investors to track the performance of distinct market segments worldwide…and might be used as a benchmark against which to measure performance." If these companies make changes to their CR programs, it represents a huge impact on society. (http://en.wikipedia.org/wiki/Russell_Indexes)

[62] **Checkbook Philanthropy** is when a company writes a check to a nonprofit without regard to alignment with long term corporate goals.

[63] **Milton Friedman:** A free-market economist: "Milton Friedman played three roles in the intellectual (and economic) life of the twentieth century. There was Friedman the economist's economist, who wrote technical, more or less apolitical analyses of consumer behavior and inflation. There was Friedman the policy entrepreneur, who spent decades campaigning on behalf of the policy known as monetarism—finally seeing the Federal Reserve and the Bank of England adopt his doctrine at the end of the 1970s, only to abandon it as unworkable a few years later. Finally, there was Friedman the ideologue, the great popularizer of free-market doctrine. (http://www.nybooks.com/articles/archives/2007/feb/15/who-was-milton-friedman/?pagination=false) He felt that the individual was responsible for charitable giving and not the corporation.

[64] IBM Smarter Planet: "Since 2008, we've talked about what it takes to build a smarter planet. We've learned that our companies, our cities and our world are complex systems-indeed, systems of systems. Advancing these systems to be more instrumented, intelligent and interconnected requires a profound shift in management and governance toward far more collaborative approaches." For an overview of IBM Smarter Planet: http://www.ibm.com/smarterplanet/us/en/overview/ideas/index.html?re=spf

[65] Fair Trade: (1) "Fair trade is a trading partnership, based on dialogue, transparency and respect, that seeks greater equity in international trade. It contributes to sustainable development by offering better trading conditions to, and securing the rights of, marginalized producers and workers – especially in the South. Fair trade organizations, backed by consumers, are engaged actively in supporting producers, awareness raising and in campaigning for changes in the rules and practice of conventional international trade." (2) Fair trade is an organized social movement and market-based approach that aims to help producers in developing countries to make better trading conditions and promote sustainability. The movement advocates the payment of a higher price to exporters as well as higher social and environmental standards. It focuses in particular on exports from developing countries to developed countries, most notably handicrafts, coffee, cocoa, sugar, tea, bananas, honey, cotton, wine, fresh fruit, chocolate, flowers and gold. (Wikipedia, http://en.wikipedia.org/wiki/Fair_trade) Wikipedia asserts in its discussion that there is insufficient data to truly calculate the benefits of Fair Trade.

[66] **NGO: Non-Governmental Organization** "is a legally constituted organization created by natural or legal persons that operates independently from any government." It's estimated that there are 40,000 international NGO's. (http://en.wikipedia.org/wiki/Non-governmental_organization).

[67] **Knowledge Workers:** "Knowledge" Workers include professionals with specific skills like accounting, marketing, technology, whose knowledge can be transferred to other organizations.

[68] Obama Presidential Campaign broke fundraising records in 2008 by attracting the small donor through e-mail, social media and online advertising. To learn about some of the lessons please see the following: "Fundraising Lessons From the Obama Campaign," Peter Panepento, July 28, 2008, The Chronicle of Philanthropy; "Election-Year Fundraising Success Holds Lessons for Charities" by Sue Hoye, June 12, 2008, The Chronicle of Philanthropy.

[69] **Contributory Consumption** is the practice of donating a specific percentage from each product purchase or from corporate net proceeds to a cause.

[70] Ariel Schwartz, Fast Company, "Patagonia, Adidas, Walmart Team Up on sustainable Apparel Coalition;" Feb. 25, 2011. **Patagonia Sustainable Apparel Coalition**: Started in 2009, this coalition is focused on developing a sustainability

222

assessment tool for apparel companies' supply chain. The coalition began when Patagonia assisted Walmart in analyzing its apparel production affect on the world. At the time, Patagonia was also developing an assessment mechanism for the Outdoor Industry Association. An assessment tool measures such indicators as energy and water use, greenhouse emissions, waste, and social labor practices. The coalition has thirty members, including companies such as Levi Strauss & Co., Marks & Spencer, REI and Nordstroms. Members share best practices and information to improve supply chain sustainability. The coalition's goal is to provide measurement tools that will lead to improved sustainable practices in the supply chain. Eventually it will provide a Sustainable Consumer Indicator for all members. It hopes to have at least 50 members by the end of 2012 and include all apparel and shoe companies as well.

[71] Let's Move Initiative - Started by Michelle Obama, this community initiative aims to improve the nutrition of children and families through how they consume food. President Obama created a Task Force on Childhood Obesity to study the issues related to this problem and establish benchmarks for achieving goals. The Task Force made five recommendation: (1) Creating a healthy start for children;(2) Empowering parents and caregivers; (3) Providing healthy food in schools; (4)Improving access to healthy, affordable foods; (5) Increasing physical activity. For more information: http://www.letsmove.gov/about

[72] Nike's Green Xchange - "The Xchange is a Web-based marketplace where companies can collaborate and share intellectual property which can lead to new sustainability business models and innovation. Ten organizations have already signed on…the exchange includes a licensing protocol." "Nike and Parterns Launch the Green Exchange," January 28, 2010, Huffington Post, http://www.huffingtonpost.com/don-tapscott/davos-nike-and-partners-1_b_441181.html;
The Green Xchange website: http://www.greenxchange.cc/info/about

[73] Product Red - According to Wikipedia, "Product Red is a brand licensed to partner companies such as Nike, American Express (UK), Apple Inc., Starbucks, Converse, Bugaboo, Penguin Classics (UK & International), Gap, Emporio Armani, Hallmark (US) and Dell. It was founded in 2006 by U2 frontman and activist Bono and Bobby Shriver of ONE/DATA to engage the private sector in raising awareness and funds to help eliminate AIDS in Africa. The Global Fund to Fight AIDS, Tuberculosis and Malaria is the recipient of (RED) monies…Each partner company creates a product with the Product Red logo. In return for the opportunity to increase its own revenue through the Product Red products that it sells, a percentage of the profit is given to the Global Fund. 100% of the funds generated by (RED) partners and events goes to Global Fund programs that provide medical care and support services for people affected by HIV/AIDS in Africa. No overhead is taken by either (RED) or the Global Fund. By 2011, it had generated $170 million to support Global Fund financed AIDS grants. These grants have reached more than 7.5 million people in Ghana, Lesotho, Rwanda, South Africa, Swaziland and Zambia." http://en.wikipedia.org/wiki/Product_Red

74 Socialvest is a shopping site that allows a percentage of everything purchased to go towards charity. It has over 600+ retailers and 1.5 million charities. https://www.socialvest.us/vision

75 Architecture for Humanity is a nonprofit design services firm founded in 1999. "We are building a more sustainable future through the power of professional design." http://architectureforhumanity.org/about

76 **Cause Integration** refers to how a company supports a cause within it's structure, either through Matching donations, Employee Engagement, Cause Marketing or direct sponsorship.

77 **Personal Fundraising Page(s)** are created for an individual conducting a personal fundraiser on behalf of a cause. Nonprofits will assist individuals in creating a personal page on behalf of a fundraising campaign for their benefit. Many websites also exist for individuals to create his/her own fundraiser (Crowdrise provides these pages to individuals).

78 **Shared Values** "Explicit or implicit fundamental beliefs, concepts, and principles that underlie the culture of an organization, and which guide decisions and behavior of its employees, management and members." From BusinessDictionary.com

79 Bill Clinton - Take to Scale or Scale Up: "One working definition of scale-up is when you have a good idea or program that (1) may have applicability elsewhere and/or (2) is of interest to others in different geographic locations. You look at ways to effectively replicate just those parts of the idea or program that are (1) core to keeping the program's integrity and/or (2) can be appropriately and effectively adapted elsewhere." http://globalscale.wikispaces.com/What+does+scale+up+mean%3F

80 **Endowment:** Can be a fund that generates income for a charity. An "endowed" gift is usually a large amount established to "inspire others and future gifts" that creates income for the charity. "The nonprofit invests the gift and uses only a portion of the interest earned to carry out the gift's purpose." An "endowed" gift is a Planned Giving" tool. (*Effective Fundraising for Nonprofits* by Illona Bray, pg 234)

81 **Capital Campaign:** Focuses on raising money for large scale projects in "which your entire organization mobilizes around a particular goal or project, like funding buildings." (*Effective Fundraising for Nonprofits* by Ilona Bray, pg. 209)

82 **Gift Planning** or **Planned Giving** is a segment of fundraising that incorporates a variety of giving tools not geared towards the direct use of cash. Often these tools enable a donor to use assets in a creative way, with tax and potential income benefits.

[83] **Military Industrial Complex** "is a concept commonly used to refer to policy and monetary relationships between legislators, national armed forces, and the defense industrial base that supports them." (http://en.wikipedia.org/wiki/Military–industrial_complex). In fundraising it's important to build relationships with many groups, donor types, and partners to help advance the cause, as big as the network represented by a Military Industrial Complex.

[84] **Annual Fund** is a yearly campaign aimed at individual supporters, usually asking for unrestricted donations.

[85] **Bequest:** Money or article left to someone in a will (Oxford American Dictionary); Nonprofits might not be aware of being the beneficiary of a bequest until a donor has passed away. These types of donations can also be known as 'Legacy' gifts.

[86] "Giving USA 2011; The Annual Report on Philanthropy for the year 2010;" Giving USA Foundation, The Center on Philanthropy at Indiana University.